ATTENTION AND MOTOR SKILL LEARNING

GABRIELE WULF, PhD

PROFESSOR

Department of Kinesiology

University of Nevada, Las Vegas

Human Kinetics

Library of Congress Cataloging-in-Publication Data

Wulf, Gabriele.
    Attention and motor skill learning / Gabriele Wulf.
        p. ; cm.
    Includes bibliographical references and index.
    ISBN-13: 978-0-7360-6270-1 (hard cover)
    ISBN-10: 0-7360-6270-X (hard cover)
1. Motor learning. 2. Attention. I. Title.
    [DNLM: 1. Motor Skills--physiology. 2. Attention--physiology. 3. Learning--physiology.
    WE 104 W961a 2007]
    BF295.W848 2007
    152.3'34--dc22

                                                                        2006103132

ISBN-10: 0-7360-6270-X

ISBN-13: 978-0-7360-6270-1

Acquisitions Editor: Judy Patterson Wright, PhD; **Developmental Editor:** Judy Park; **Assistant Editor:** Lee Alexander; **Copyeditor:** Joyce Sexton; **Proofreader:** Kathy Bennett; **Indexer:** Bobbi Swanson; **Permission Manager:** Dalene Reeder; **Graphic Designer:** Nancy Rasmus; **Graphic Artist:** Angela K. Snyder; **Photo Manager:** Laura Fitch; **Cover Designer:** Bob Reuther; **Photographer (cover):** © Photodisc; **Art Manager:** Kelly Hendren; **Illustrator:** Tammy Page; **Printer:** Edwards Brothers Malloy

Printed in the United States of America   10 9 8 7 6 5

The paper in this book is certified under a sustainable forestry program.

Human Kinetics
P.O. Box 5076
Champaign, IL 61825-5076
Website: www.HumanKinetics.com

In the United States, email info@hkusa.com or call 800-747-4457.
In Canada, email info@hkcanada.com.
In the United Kingdom/Europe, email hk@hkeurope.com.

For information about Human Kinetics' coverage in other areas of the world,
please visit our website: **www.HumanKinetics.com**

E3643

To my mom, Marianne, the memory of my dad, Hubert, and my brother, Michael, for their unconditional love and support

CONTENTS

PREFACE

An individual's focus of attention can have a significant influence on the performance of motor skills. What a person directs his or her attention to while executing a skill determines how fluid the motion is, how consistent the movement is, how accurate the outcome is, and, in general, how well the skill is performed. In fact, it has been known for a long time that paying "too much attention" to one's actions can disrupt performance, especially if the skill is well practiced. For example, simply being observed while we perform a routine task such as typing on a computer keyboard has the effect, more often than not, of making us focus more on our actions. The result of paying more attention to hitting the right keys and trying to avoid typos is typically that we produce *more* typos than usual.

What is the reason for this? Why is it that when we concentrate on what we are doing, the fluency that normally characterizes our movements is gone and we make mistakes that we normally don't make? There is hardly an athlete or musician who could not give an example of "choking," especially when he or she was trying hard to do well. Performance decrements that occur when we consciously direct our attention to the coordination of our movements are very common.

Perhaps even more interestingly, new research shows that the *learning* of new motor skills also suffers when we direct attention to the coordination of our movements. This contrasts with the view of most people, including many scientists, coaches, and physical therapists. According to traditional views, people have to go through a learning stage in which they consciously control their movements. But if conscious control is detrimental, the question arises: Is it possible to learn a new skill without directing conscious attention to the coordination of our body movements? Can we somehow bypass the first "conscious" stage of learning? Or is there a way to at least shorten this stage and speed up the learning process?

These are the issues this book addresses. The book explores how a person's focus of attention affects motor performance, and in particular the learning of motor skills. In the past few years, considerable research has been directed toward examining the effects that the type of attentional focus has on motor performance and learning, and toward understanding the mechanisms underlying these effects. The goal of this book is to provide a synthesis of the knowledge that has resulted from this research. It is by no means a complete account of attention and motor performance. Rather, the book is based on findings of experimental studies that have specifically addressed the effects of a performer's focus of attention on motor performance or learning.

AUDIENCE

This book should be useful to anyone with an interest in human motor control and learning. Students of kinesiology, psychology, sport sciences, physical education, physical or occupational therapy, or the performing arts, as well as practitioners working in these and related fields, will benefit from a better understanding of how and why a person's focus of attention influences the learning (or relearning) of motor skills. Not only does the research discussed in this book advance our understanding of the role of attention in motor performance; the findings also have important practical implications. They suggest simple yet powerful ways to enhance motor skill learning by directing the learner's attention. The results have relevance for any practical setting in which effective and efficient training of motor skills is a concern.

ORGANIZATION

The book begins with an overview of traditional and more recent views of how attention should be directed as an individual progresses through the stages of learning, or from beginner to expert (chapter 1). Views differ with respect to what novices should direct their attention to while practicing a motor skill. Whereas many believe that beginners need to focus on the coordination of their movements (what has been labeled "internal focus" of attention), new research findings suggest that this type of focus can actually hamper the learning process.

Chapter 2 introduces a potential solution to the problem of performance decrements caused by an internal focus. It will be shown that giving learners instructions that direct their attention to the *effects* of their movements on the "environment," such as an implement (i.e., inducing a so-called external focus), facilitates the learning process. Chapter 3 deals with another important learning variable, namely the feedback provided to learners, and shows how the attentional focus induced by feedback influences learning. The findings discussed in this chapter not only have important practical implications; they also challenge current theoretical views of feedback.

As the informed reader will want to know not only *that* a certain type of focus "works," but also *how* or *why* it works, chapter 4 deals with possible reasons for the differential effects of an internal versus an external attentional focus. Neurophysiological and psychological correlates of different attentional foci are described, and an explanation for the advantages of adopting an external focus is provided. The benefits of an external focus extend to a wide variety of skills and populations.

The discussion in chapter 5 centers on whether and how the optimal type of focus might change with the individual's level of expertise. Even though research in this particular area is still relatively sparse, there are indications that as an individual gains more experience, his or her focus of attention should change as well in order to optimize performance. This chapter includes discussion of how and why the optimal focus is assumed to change.

Chapter 6 focuses on so-called suprapostural activities (e.g., juggling on an unstable surface). These skills are particularly interesting, as the type of focus on the suprapostural task not only influences suprapostural performance, but also indirectly affects postural control.

Chapter 7 reviews findings related to how the attentional focus affects the performance of special populations, including children, older individuals, and those with impairments such as Parkinson's disease.

SPECIAL FEATURES

Each chapter in this book starts with an **Opening Scenario,** a short narrative or a situation that presents a motor learning problem and the role of attention focusing in solving it. These scenarios frame the concepts in the chapter in a practical manner. In each chapter you will also find **Attentional Insights,** sections that reflect what performers are thinking as they execute a particular motor skill.

To facilitate the application of research findings, examples for various sport and rehabilitation settings are given in a **Practical**

Applications section at the end of each chapter. This feature presents an applied topic with relevant tasks and discussion questions. Many of these questions are open-ended and should elicit inspired debate.

In some areas, the evidence for certain phenomena is not as strong as would be desirable, and in others, research studies are still scarce or lacking altogether. Each chapter ends with **Future Directions** for research, highlighting questions that still need to be answered.

Ten years of research on the effects of internal versus external foci of attention have produced some interesting findings. There can be no doubt that how well we perform and learn motor skills depends to a great extent on what we focus our attention on. Directing attention to the movement effect typically results in superior performance than directing attention to the actual coordination of the body movements. The influence of the attentional focus on performance is sometimes almost immediate. But, more importantly, the type of focus an individual adopts while practicing a skill affects the whole learning process. Not only is a higher level of performance often achieved faster with an external relative to an internal focus, but the skill is better retained. That is, more effective performance is seen even after retention intervals—when no focus reminders are given, and sometimes even when the individual is prevented from adopting the same focus. Furthermore, the advantages of an external focus are generalizable to a wide variety of skills and skill levels and have been found for young adults, as well as for children, older individuals and those with physical impairments. We also have a relatively good understanding of how a person's focus of attention affects his or her performance. As already noted, there is pretty good evidence indicating that the adoption of an external compared to an internal focus results in greater automaticity in the control of movements.

Whether you are a coach, instructor, professional or recreational athlete, dancer, musician or music teacher, physical or occupational therapist, someone with a physical impairment, or perhaps someone who is trying to learn a new sport skill, I hope that this book will help you improve your performance, or at least make physical activity more enjoyable for you. If nothing else, I hope it will have increased your appreciation of the motor system's automatic control capabilities. If we trust our motor system to do its job, it is more likely to do that job than if we interfere with it by trying to exert control over it.

I hope that you will find the effects that our attentional focus has on our performance as fascinating as I do.

ACKNOWLEDGMENTS

Many people have contributed to this book. Acquisitions editor Judy Wright and developmental editor Judy Park have provided numerous invaluable suggestions that have greatly enhanced the readability and visual appeal of the book. I also appreciate the excellent work of copyeditor Joyce Sexton and assistant editor Lee Alexander. Many thanks to Adina Mornell, Bill Prinzmetal, and Geralyn Schulz, who provided interesting *Attentional Insights* based on their professional experience and expertise. The research presented in this book would not have been possible without the collaborative support of many colleagues. In particular, Nancy McNevin and Charlie Shea have been instrumental in advancing the theoretical framework. They also conducted several of the experiments reported in this book. I am grateful to Merrill Landers, John Mercer, Wolfgang Prinz, and Tonya Toole for their important contributions to a number of studies. Of course, research is almost impossible without the assistance of dedicated graduate students. I would like to acknowledge the involvement of my former students in Germany: Thomas Fuchs, Markus Höß, Matthias Gärtner, Sabine Lauterbach, Florian Ritter, Andreas Schwarz, Thomas Töllner, Sebastian Wächter, Stefan Wortmann; in England: Nathan McConnel, Damian Poulter, Vaso Totsika, Matthias Weigelt; and in the United States: Carolina Granados, Jiang Su, Jason Vance, and Tiffany Zachry. Finally, my deepest appreciation goes to Nancy McNevin not only for her collaboration, but also for her continued moral support and unfailing good advice.

© Getty Images

Learning to ice-skate is challenging. In the early stages, learners tend to control their movements consciously and thus adopt a stiff posture in attempts to maintain their balance.

CHAPTER 1

ATTENTIONAL FOCUS AND THE LEARNING PROCESS

As we practice motor skills, such as catching baseballs, shooting free throws, riding a bicycle, hitting golf balls, or skiing down a slope, we typically observe certain changes. Not only do we get better at what we are doing—we hit the golf balls closer to the hole, or fall less frequently on the ski slopes—but our performance also becomes more consistent and less dependent on "luck." In addition, we are able to perform the skill with less muscular effort as we develop a more efficient technique. Through practice we learn to produce the appropriate forces at the right time and in the appropriate directions. In addition, we learn to avoid unnecessary cocontractions of agonist and antagonist muscles. As a consequence, less and less energy is needed, and we don't get tired as quickly. Somebody learning to ice-skate, for example, tends to contract most of her leg muscles, and even the muscles of her upper body, thus increasing the stiffness of the joints in an attempt to maintain balance. In addition, the learner frequently shifts her weight from one leg to the other, often skating on both legs at the same time. As a result, she does not produce much forward momentum, but still uses considerable energy just to remain in an upright position. With increasing experience, she learns to skate on one leg for longer periods of time, to relax muscle groups that are not essential, and to produce forces that propel her forward.

We also learn to exploit passive forces, such as gravity and Coriolis forces (Gentile, 1998). Early in the learning process, passive forces are not utilized very effectively. In fact, cocontractions, which supposedly give us more "control" over our actions, also decrease the influence of passive forces. With practice, however, the coordination of active and passive forces becomes more finely tuned, and we increasingly learn to utilize those external forces, thereby saving additional energy (Bernstein, 1967; Gentile, 1998). For example, when we swing a tennis racket or golf club, gravitational and Coriolis forces can be used to increase the speed of the motion without additional muscular energy.

In addition to the reduced muscular effort that results from practice, less and less mental effort is required to perform the skill. We don't need to pay as much attention to what we are doing as we did early in the learning process. The control of the movement becomes more automatic, and we can pay more attention to other things, such as the strategy in a ball game, the terrain in cross country running or skiing, or the artistic expression in dance or gymnastics.

Almost everything we do requires at least some attention. This includes the performance of motor skills. In fact, what we direct our attention to determines to a large extent how well we perform and learn motor skills. This chapter first looks at the different stages of learning, then more specifically focuses on how the role of attention changes as we gain experience with a certain skill. In particular, we will consider different views of how attention should be directed in order to optimize learning. Many researchers and practitioners believe that it is necessary for novices to focus on the coordination of their movements. Yet there is also evidence to suggest that this is not very beneficial, or that it can even hamper the learning process. Therefore, some researchers have developed approaches that aim to prevent the detrimental effects of focusing on one's movements. In contrast to the controversial views regarding the teaching and learning of motor skills in novices, there is general agreement that the performance of experts suffers when their attention is directed to the details of their movements. This often happens when an individual performs in a stressful situation. Here an important question is whether "choking" under pressure can be reduced, or even prevented, by focusing attention appropriately.

MOTOR SKILL LEARNING STAGES

Even though motor skills vary widely in type and complexity, the learning process that individuals go through when acquiring various motor skills is similar. Paul Fitts (1964; Fitts & Posner, 1967) has proposed three stages (or phases) of learning: the cognitive, associative, and autonomous stages (see table 1.1). The cognitive stage is characterized by the learner's trying to figure out what exactly needs to be done. Considerable cognitive activity is typically required in this stage, in which movements are controlled in a relatively conscious manner. Because learners sometimes use (overt or covert) self-talk, this stage has also been labeled the "verbal stage" (Adams, 1971). During this phase, learners often experiment with different strategies to find out which ones work or don't work in bringing them closer to the movement goal. Also, learners tend to pay attention to the step-by-step execution of the skill, which requires considerable attentional capacity. The result of using conscious control strategies is that the movement is relatively slow, abrupt, and inefficient and that performance is rather inconsistent.

Once the learner has acquired the basic movement pattern, the second, or associative, phase of learning begins. This phase is characterized by more subtle movement adjustments. The movement

TABLE 1.1   STAGES OF LEARNING

Stages of learning	Characteristics	Attentional demands
Cognitive (verbal)	Movements are slow, inconsistent, and inefficient. Considerable cognitive activity is required.	Large parts of the movement are controlled consciously.
Associative	Movements are more fluid, reliable, and efficient. Less cognitive activity is required.	Some parts of the movement are controlled consciously, some automatically.
Autonomous (motor)	Movements are accurate, consistent, and efficient. Little or no cognitive activity is required.	Movement is largely controlled automatically.

Adapted from R.N. Singer 1988.

3

outcome is more reliable, and the movements are more consistent from trial to trial. Inefficient cocontractions are gradually reduced, and the movement becomes more economical. In addition, at least parts of the movement are controlled more automatically, and more attention can be directed to other aspects of performance.

After extensive practice, the performer reaches the autonomous phase (termed "motor stage" by Adams [1971]), which is characterized by fluent and seemingly effortless motions. Movements are not only accurate, with few or no errors, but also very consistent. In addition, movement production is very efficient and requires relatively little muscular energy. The skill is performed largely automatically at this stage, and movement execution requires little or no attention.

Thus, one thing that seems to change considerably as we gain more experience with a skill is the amount of attention that we need to dedicate to its execution. Some studies have looked more closely at how attentional demands change as individuals go through different phases of learning, and these are reviewed next. We will also see how the performance of motor skills is affected at different stages of expertise as a function of what individuals direct their attention to.

ATTENTIONAL RESOURCES

As already described, the attentional resources that need to be directed to the planning and execution of a skill are assumed to be reduced as performers progress through the different stages of learning. One way to test this assumption experimentally is to have individuals perform a so-called secondary task in conjunction with the motor skill of interest. This way, researchers can determine how much interference the secondary task creates. If the "primary" skill—that is, the skill that the researcher is interested in—is controlled relatively automatically, its performance should not be affected very much by the simultaneous performance of the secondary task. In contrast, in the early stages of learning, when presumably more attention needs to be directed to the execution of the skill, having to perform a secondary task at the same time would be expected to take away necessary attentional resources and degrade the performance of the primary task. Jack Leavitt, a Canadian psychologist, was the first to demonstrate this. In one of his studies (Leavitt, 1979), novice and experienced ice hockey players were required to skate and stick-handle a puck through a slalom course. Under one condition, they had to perform an additional task, namely, identifying geometrical shapes that were projected onto a screen. The secondary task requirement did not affect the skating and stick-handling performance in experts. However, skating speed was reduced for novice players when they had to perform the secondary task. Another study showed similar results for dribbling soccer balls (Smith & Chamberlin, 1992): The performance of experienced soccer players dribbling a soccer ball through a series of pylons was not hampered when they had to perform a visual monitoring task at the same time. Novice soccer players, in contrast, showed a clear performance decrement under the dual-task condition compared to when they performed the dribbling task by itself. Similarly, Bruce Abernethy (1988) showed that, whereas novice badminton players made more errors when they had to react to an auditory probe while playing, experts did not. These

© Getty Images

An experienced hockey player is able to direct his attention to the actions of opponents or teammates, rather than his own skating and stick-handling.

findings suggest that while "skill-focused" attention is presumably necessary early in learning, its role diminishes as learning progresses and performance becomes more automated.

This phenomenon is also supported by interviews of novice and expert golfers. When novices were asked to recall the steps they went through during their last putt, they remembered *more* details than did expert golfers (Beilock & Carr, 2001). Even though, not surprisingly, experts generally knew more about the correct movement technique than novices did, they apparently had less access to how exactly they performed a particular putt. The fact that experts' memory for a particular movement is less detailed than that of novices is in line with the view that novices consciously control their movements whereas experts devote little, if any, attention to the execution of the skill.

Most people, including many scientists, assume that novices, in contrast to experts, need to pay attention to the step-by-step execution of the skill (e.g., Beilock & Carr, 2004; Gray, 2004; Meinel & Schnabel, 1976). As a consequence, they believe that instructions directing novices' attention to the coordination of their movements should be beneficial. In the next section, we will examine the evidence for the view that novices need to direct their attention to the execution of their movements. As it turns out, there does not appear to be much support for this view that a "skill focus" (at least one that involves attention directed to the execution of the movement) is very effective, even in the early stages of learning. There is little disagreement that once an individual has reached the autonomous stage, in which movements are usually controlled automatically, paying attention to skill execution is typically detrimental. In the section, "Expert Motor Learning and Performance" on page 15, we will take a look at some evidence for this phenomenon, including instances of "choking under pressure." We will see what exactly happens when experts, for one reason or another, direct their attention to the execution of the skill, and how this affects their performance.

NOVICE MOTOR LEARNING AND PERFORMANCE

It is generally assumed that novices benefit from information about how to best perform a motor skill. After all, they need to get an idea of the correct movement. Therefore, the traditional belief is that learning during the early stages is enhanced when learners are made aware of their movements and of how they are performing in relation to the goal movement. To facilitate the learning process, instructions and feedback are typically given that direct learners' attention to various aspects of their movement coordination. That such instructions promote the use of conscious modes of control is not viewed as problematic, but rather as a necessary phase that the learner must go through in order to reach the stage in which movement control is more or less automatic. After all, the purpose of instructions and feedback that teachers or coaches give is to guide the learner toward the correct movement and to avoid the need to make changes in the technique later when the pattern of coordination has already become stabilized. But are these instructions really helpful? In the following section, we will take a look at studies that have examined how instructions directing learners' attention to various aspects of the task (or away from the task) affect their performance.

INSTRUCTION AND FEEDBACK

Several studies have addressed how directing learners' attention to the execution of the skill affects performance, as compared to preventing them from focusing on the skill (by having them perform a secondary task) or not giving them focus instructions. For example, Gray (2004) used a baseball simulation study in which participants (novices and experts) swung a bat at a simulated approaching baseball. Novices had smaller timing errors when they focused on batting (skill-focused condition) compared to when they focused on an unrelated task. Thus, not surprisingly, "distracting" them by requiring them to perform an unrelated task at the same time degraded their performance. Yet the instructions that directed their attention to the mechanics of the motor task (skill-focused condition) did not provide a benefit relative to having them perform without an additional task (single-task condition).

Similar results were found in the golf putting study by Beilock and colleagues (2004), in which participants had to detect a target tone (dual-task condition) or were asked to focus on a straight club motion (skill-focused condition). Even though novices showed more effective performance when they focused on the golf club motion, rather than the tone, novices did not benefit from the instructions that directed their attention to the skill, relative to a single-task condition. This was the case even though the single-task condition was performed first (as in Gray's [2004] study). That is, despite the additional amount of practice participants had received by the time they performed under the skill-focused condition, there was no significant improvement.

Finally, in the soccer dribbling study by Beilock and colleagues (2002), novices generally performed more effectively, that is, needed less time to complete the course, in the skill-focus condition (focus on the feet) compared to the dual-task condition (monitoring a list of words). Also, the skill-focus condition resulted in better performance relative to a single-task condition. This result has to be viewed with caution, though, as the single-task condition was again performed first, and the improved performance in the skill-focus condition could also reflect a practice effect. In fact, in a very similar study by Ford and colleagues (2005), in which the order of conditions was randomized, no performance benefits were found when the attention of novices was directed to their feet compared to when they performed under a single-task condition.

At least from these studies, there does not seem to be any convincing evidence that directing novices' attention to the execution of the skill is indeed beneficial. Conclusions such as "it may be beneficial to direct performers' attention to step-by-step components of a skill early in the stages of acquisition" (Beilock et al., 2002, p. 15), therefore, might be a little overstated.

Moreover, there is even evidence that the performance of beginners can suffer when they are given instructions about the correct technique (Wulf & Weigelt, 1997). This experiment used a ski simulator task. The ski simulator consists of two bowed rails and a platform on wheels that is attached to the ski simulator by elastic rubber belts. The rubber belts ensure that the platform returns to the center position. The platform can be made to move sideways on the rails if force is exerted on it.

We gave participants (who had never performed the task before) instructions about the correct technique. That is, we informed them before they started practicing the ski simulator task when to exert force on the platform. Another group was not given this information; rather, they were free to discover the correct technique for themselves. Across three days of practice, it became clear that the instructions were actually not helping (see figure 1.1). Not only that, those participants who were given the "benefit" of information about how to correctly perform the task made clearly less progress than participants who were not given this information. At the end of the practice phase, the *noninstructed* group showed a clear per-

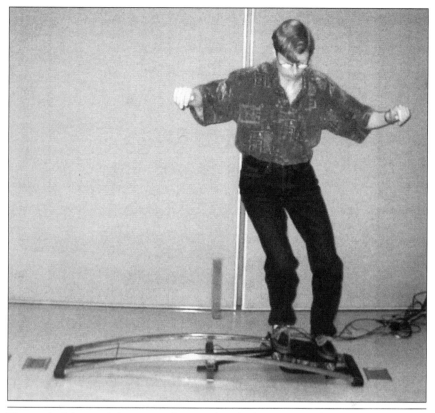

The goal of the participant standing on the platform is to make oscillatory movements with the largest possible amplitudes and to move as fast as possible.

formance advantage. Moreover, we tried to create a somewhat more stressful situation on the very last trial by telling participants that they would now be observed by a ski expert, who would evaluate their performance. As can be seen from figure 1.1, the differences between groups even increased slightly on this "stress" test. Thus, the noninstructed group tended to have an even greater advantage, compared to the instructed group, when the pressure to perform well was increased.

This finding does not appear to be a coincidence. Another study, in which a very different motor task was used, showed similar benefits of *not* giving learners instructions about how to perform the task (Hodges & Lee, 1999). The task was a complex bimanual coordination task. Specifically, participants had to move two handles, which were attached to slides, back and forth in the horizontal plane, with one hand following the other by a quarter of a cycle. If performed

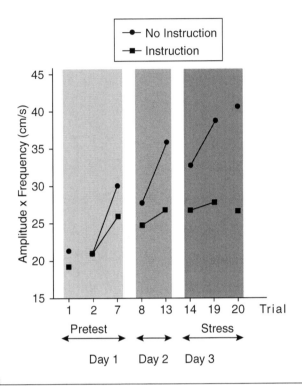

FIGURE 1.1 Overall performance (amplitude × frequency) of the groups with and without instructions on the pretest (Trial 1) and on the first (second on Day 1) and last trial of each day (Trials 2, 7, 8, 13, 14, 20) in the ski simulator study with novices by Wulf and Weigelt (1997, Experiment 1).

correctly, this motion created a circle pattern on a computer screen. (If one hand lagged the other by more or less than a quarter of a cycle, an elliptical pattern would result.) Different groups of participants were given (specific or general) instructions about how to coordinate their hand movements in order to produce a circle pattern. Another group, however, was simply instructed to produce a circle. That is, these people were left to their own devices and had to figure out themselves what they had to do to create the circle. The most interesting finding was one seen on a transfer test after two days of practice. On this test, an attention-demanding task was added, which required participants to produce the circle while counting backward by threes. The results showed that the group that had *not* been given instructions performed more effectively than the groups that had received instructions about the correct coordination pattern. This result is similar to the findings of the ski simulator study already described (Wulf & Weigelt, 1997). It demonstrates that the performance of the instructed groups was hampered when they had to direct their attention to the secondary (counting) task, whereas the noninstructed group learned the task better *and* was able to perform it with a greater degree of automaticity.

What is happening here? Why do instructions that would be assumed to benefit performance and learning have detrimental effects? While there is general agreement that experts' performance is negatively affected when they direct their attention to the details of their movements, there is less agreement when it comes to novices. Even though many researchers and practitioners believe that it is necessary for novices to direct their attention to the execution of their movements, these studies suggest that instructions inducing "self-focused" attention can actually hamper the learning of motor skills in novices. Considering that instructions given in sport, music, or physical therapy, for example, typically direct individuals' attention to skill execution, and more specifically to the coordination of their movements, these results are quite worrisome. Why do instructions not help as much as we expect them to? And perhaps most importantly, are there ways to not only avoid the detrimental effects of instructions but to *enhance* learning?

ADJUSTING ATTENTIONAL FOCUS

In the mid-1980s, Robert Singer, a sport psychology professor at the University of Florida, argued that instructing learners to be consciously aware of their body movements during the execution of a skill might not be very effective (e.g., Singer, 1985, 1988). On the basis of anecdotal evidence suggesting that expert performers typically do not think about the details of their actions when executing a skill (e.g., Gallwey, 1982; Garfield & Bennett, 1985), Singer argued that one way to help beginners attain such a state of automaticity might be to use an instructional approach that distracts learners from their own movements. Because attempting to perform a movement skill as if it were automatic did not appear to be tenable for beginners, though, Singer developed his Five-Step Approach as a compromise between "awareness" and "nonawareness" strategies. Before executing a skill, performers are instructed to attain an optimal emotional state (step 1) and go though the motion mentally (step 2). Step 3 involves "focusing," in which the performer is supposed to concentrate on one relevant cue (e.g., the seams of a tennis ball, the dimples of a golf ball, the target) and to think only of this cue to block out all other thoughts. Step 4 requires the performer to execute the movement while not thinking about the act itself or the possible outcome. The last step (step 5) involves assessing the outcome and planning adjustments for the next trial, if time permits. Thus, even though "awareness" components are used in this approach, as the performer is asked to imagine the act *before* executing it, the important point is that external cues are used to prevent the performer from focusing on the movement during its execution.

Singer's Five-Step Approach

1. *Readying:* Think positively as to performance expectations; attain an optimal attitudinal-emotional state; attempt to do things in preparation for performance that are associated with previous best performances; try to attain consistency as to preparatory mechanics.

2. *Imaging:* Briefly mentally picture performing the act—how it should be done, and how you can do it at your very best; visualize from the results of the act to its initiation; feel the movement.

3. *Focusing:* Concentrating intensely on one relevant feature of the situation, such as the seams of a tennis ball to be hit, think only of this cue, which will block out all other thoughts.

4. *Executing:* Do it when you feel you are ready; do not think of anything about the act itself or the possible outcome.

5. *Evaluating:* If time permits, use the available feedback to learn from; assess the performance outcome and the effectiveness of each step in the routine; adjust any procedure next time, if necessary.

From Singer, 1988.

A number of studies have shown that the Five-Step Approach can be relatively effective (e.g., Singer et al., 1991; Singer, Lidor, & Cauraugh, 1993). Specifically, compared to not giving learners attentional focus instructions (control conditions), the Five-Step Approach has been demonstrated to result in improved performance and learning (e.g., Kim, Singer, & Radlo, 1996). However, when compared to what happened in a "nonawareness" condition, in which participants were simply informed to preplan the movement and focus on a single cue (e.g., the target in a throwing task), no additional advantage of going through the five steps was seen (Singer, Lidor, & Cauraugh, 1993).

It should be pointed out that Singer makes a distinction between a "learning" focus and a "performance" focus. He suggests that it might be appropriate for advanced performers to just concentrate on one cue and let the body take care of the rest. However, he believes that for beginners, it might be more effective to direct their attention to important aspects of the skill, such as the proper follow-through upon stroking the ball, or the weight shift while hitting the baseball (Singer, 1988). Even though this makes performers aware of certain features of the movement, Singer assumes that the attainment of automaticity is a gradual process and that such instructions are not detrimental.

One drawback of Singer's Five-Step Approach is that it is limited to self-paced skills. These are skills that are not performed under time pressure, so that the performer has enough time to go through the steps while getting ready; and the environment in which such skills are performed is stable and predictable. Of course, many sport skills do not afford the performer this luxury. How should we practice skills that require fast reactions to oncoming balls (e.g., tennis, baseball, basketball, soccer), to rapid changes in the environment (e.g., moguls in skiing), or to moves by opponents (e.g., wrestling, boxing)? What should we focus our attention on when practicing and performing those types of skills? While Singer's approach might be useful for some skills, its applicability is limited.

Other scientists have taken a somewhat more radical stance than Singer. Richard Masters (1992) has also suggested that it is important *not* to think about the movement while executing it, but he goes further by arguing that instructions given to performers attempting to learn a new skill should be reduced to a minimum (e.g., Masters, 1992; Maxwell, Masters, & Eves, 2000; Singer, 1985, 1988). Masters and colleagues contend that, when given too many instructions, learners are more likely to adopt a controlled mode of information processing and tend to become preoccupied with thoughts about how they are executing the skill, which is assumed to be detrimental to performance. Therefore, making learners aware of their movements (or inducing an explicit mode of learning) should be avoided as much as possible. If the learner is allowed to acquire the skill implicitly, he or she is less likely to engage in conscious thought processes that could interfere with the automatic execution of the movement. This is assumed to be especially advantageous under stressful conditions, as in a competition, since under such conditions performers tend to "reinvest" controlled processing, with the result that performance suffers because the automatic functioning of the movement is disrupted (Masters, Polman, & Hammond, 1993).

In a number of studies, Masters and colleagues have examined these assumptions and demonstrated that there might indeed be some advantage to learning motor skills without explicit knowledge of the proper technique. For example, Masters (1992; see also Hardy, Mullen, & Jones, 1996) found that preventing learners who were practicing a golf putting task from acquiring explicit rules was beneficial to performance under stress, compared to providing learners with specific instructions about how to putt. Masters and colleagues (Masters, Polman, & Hammond, 1993) also argued that some people might have a predisposition toward the reinvestment of conscious control processes, which should make them more likely to choke in stressful situations. This notion was confirmed in studies showing that individuals who acquired more rules during practice—even when not given specific instructions about the correct technique—demonstrated less effective performance than those who reported fewer rules (e.g., Maxwell, Masters, & Eves, 2000; Masters, Polman, & Hammond, 1993).

Thus, one thing these findings suggest is that using explicit knowledge to consciously control one's movements during skill execution is not very effective. But is the optimal solution to this problem of how motor skills should be taught *not* to give learners instructions about the technique, and to actually prevent them from acquiring explicit knowledge (so that they cannot reinvest it later)? Should we really rely on learners' ability to discover the correct movement pattern, and hope that they will learn a more effective technique when we withhold information from them? Can we expect somebody to learn pole-vaulting without knowledge about the correct technique?

In fact, what the research findings show is that, even though "implicit" learners typically demonstrate less of a performance decrement in stressful situations compared to the end of practice, they hardly ever show more effective performance than "explicit" learners in those stressful situations; often, the explicit learning groups even tend to outperform the implicit learning groups on those tests (e.g., Hardy, Mullen, & Jones, 1996; Masters, 1992; Maxwell, Masters, & Eves, 2000). Of course, the critical question for most applied settings is how well people perform in test situations. How well did their training prepare them for competitions in sport, concerts in music, daily activities after occupational therapy, or rescue missions in dangerous situations? From this perspective, how people perform in practice, and how their practice performance compares to their test performance, seems rather irrelevant. What "counts" is their test performance.

Thus, it appears that we are in a dilemma when it comes to teaching motor skills: Giving novices instructions that direct their attention to the coordination of their movements is less than optimal, and previous approaches designed to prevent the negative effects of attention directed to the movement details are not without drawbacks. How can we solve this conundrum? As we will see in the following chapters, there is a relatively simple solution to this problem and an effective way of directing novices' attention so that learning is actually facilitated. First, however, we will take a look at how experts' performance—which is typically controlled relatively automatically—is affected when they direct their attention to the control of their movements. This often happens involuntarily when the individual is under pressure to perform well. As we will see, the result is often the opposite of what was intended: Performance suffers. This leads to an important question: Is there a way to reduce the detrimental effects of self-focused attention, a phenomenon sometimes called choking?

EXPERT MOTOR LEARNING AND PERFORMANCE

Choking is a common phenomenon when athletes have to perform under pressure. Yet, even in situations that don't induce stress, a person's performance might suddenly be affected negatively by other factors, including simple comments or questions about his or her technique, or even instructions given with the intention to *improve* performance! While there is plenty of anecdotal evidence for choking under pressure, scientists have also induced choking through experimental manipulations in an attempt to understand exactly how pressure, stress, anxiety, and simple "tips" or instructions affect the performance of experienced individuals. One goal of this research is to develop training methods that make performers "immune" to choking. Some of the findings related to these issues are discussed next.

CHOKING UNDER PRESSURE

When much is at stake and an athlete tries very hard to do the best he or she can, the result is often less than the athlete had hoped for and sometimes a disaster. At the 2002 Winter Olympics in Salt Lake City, 16-year-old Sarah Hughes from Long Island, New York, unexpectedly reached the finals of the women's figure skating competition after being in fourth place following the short program. Being under no pressure to actually win, she demonstrated the performance of her life. Her skate was flawless, featuring seven triple jumps. As she reported later, when she went on the ice she just wanted to "have fun." In contrast, Michelle Kwan, who was the clear favorite and was expected to win gold, was under tremendous pressure, as she had to perform after Hughes. This pressure was presumably the reason for her choking: Kwan double-footed an early triple jump, then struggled to maintain her confidence during the rest of her program, and even fell on a later triple flip. Kwan ended up with a bronze medal. Sarah Hughes won the gold medal.

The "yips" in golf putting are also a phenomenon that is often attributed to choking. Sometimes called "twitches," "jitters," or "jerks," these are involuntary hand movements that negatively affect putting, even—or especially—in experienced golfers. The yips occur mainly during tournaments or competitions, that is, in situations of increased pressure. Golfers who experience the yips tend to show increased muscular activity in the wrist muscles as well as faster heart rates. This suggests that it is the stress experienced in certain situations that causes this phenomenon, rather than underlying neurological problems. Similar pressure-induced effects on motor coordination are seen in other athletes, artists, musicians, and even physicians and dentists.

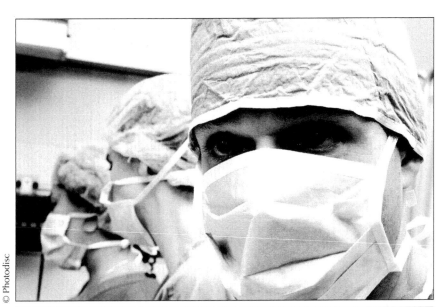

© Photodisc

The "yips" are not only a common phenomenon in sports, but also in other high-pressure situations such as surgery.

Excessive pressure not only can affect the performance of individuals negatively, but can even degrade the performance of whole teams. Baumeister and Steinhilber (1984) analyzed championship games in baseball and basketball over several decades and found that the home-field advantage can actually turn into a *disadvantage* when the pressure becomes too high. In contrast to early games in the baseball World Series or in the basketball playoff series, which home teams were indeed more likely to win, in close matches toward the end of the series the home teams lost the decisive games more often than they won! That this was due to choking on the part of the home team, and not to improvement on the part of the visiting team, was corroborated by the number of fielding errors and foul shot misses made by the home teams. Even though these errors and misses are uninfluenced by the opponent, they increased by several percentage points in the final games.

ATTENTIONAL INSIGHTS

Harold Levitt (1910-2006) played for the Harlem Globetrotters for 4 1/2 years, but he was most famous for his free-throw skills. His mother called him "Bunny" because he was short (5 ft 4 in. or 163 cm) and quick. Because of his height, Bunny was also fouled a lot. Therefore, as a child, he practiced foul shooting for hours and hours, right after finishing his homework. His effort paid off. Levitt entered tournaments and won city, state, and world championships. The contest he is best remembered for was held on April 6, 1935, in Madison Square Garden, organized by the Amateur Athletic Union. In this foul shooting contest, Levitt dunked a record 499 consecutive free throws. But he missed the 500th shot. In an interview with *Ocala Life Magazine* he said, "I must have choked."

Harold Levitt, a sharpshooter with the Harlem Globetrotters, sank 499 consecutive free throws in a basketball contest.

© Ocala Magazine/Djamel E. Ramoul

What it is that makes people choke? Some scientists believe that pressure to perform well creates distractions (e.g., Easterbrook, 1959; Wine, 1971; for a review, see Baumeister & Showers, 1986). That is, individuals tend to either miss cues that are relevant for the task or focus on things that are irrelevant to the task, including worries about their performance and the possible consequences. Such distracting thoughts are assumed to be the reason for poor performance under pressure. While distraction might be one factor responsible for these performance decrements, there is also evidence that choking is the result of people's becoming self-conscious and too concerned with the step-by-step execution of the task (e.g., Baumeister, 1984, 1985; Lewis & Linder, 1997). Self-focused attention is assumed to disrupt the automaticity in movement control that typically characterizes skilled performance. As a consequence, performance suffers or breaks down completely. Richard Masters (2000; see also Masters, Polman, & Hammond, 1993) termed this idea the "conscious processing hypothesis." The use of conscious control processes induced by stress, anxiety, or pressure to perform well reflects a temporary regress to earlier stages of learning (Pijpers, Oudejans, & Bakker, 2005), in which performance is rather volatile.

Some experimental evidence for this view comes from the baseball simulation study by Gray (2004). Gray looked at the number of judgment errors that expert batters made regarding the direction of the bat (up or down) when a tone was presented. He predicted that participants would make more judgment errors when they were in a good phase of batting performance and fewer judgment errors when they were in a batting slump. This interesting prediction was based on the assumption that, when the movements are controlled automatically and performance is at a high level, individuals should not be aware of the details of their movements (see also Beilock & Carr, 2001); therefore, judgment errors should be higher. In contrast, when individuals were in a slump, the perceived pressure to improve performance was expected to result in increased self-consciousness and a more conscious mode of control; as a consequence, it was assumed that judgment errors would be reduced. This is indeed what Gray found. There was a significant positive correlation ($r = .89$) between the number of hits and judgment errors. This indicated that at high levels of performance, the batters paid less attention to the details of the execution of the skill. When they were in a slump, however, self-focused attention increased, presumably as a result of attempts to improve. Of course, it is also possible that the slumps were created by an increase in self-focused attention that occurred for some other reason. Whatever the causal factor, though, it is interesting to see that good performance is indeed associated with less attention directed at the details of that performance.

Interestingly, it does not seem to matter whether an individual perceives pressure to improve based on his or her current performance or whether the pressure is induced by some external source. In another experiment, Gray (2004) created a pressure situation by informing participants that they would receive $20 if they were able to increase the number of hits by 15%. This condition resulted in poorer batting performance and lower judgment errors (with regard to the direction of the bat at the time a tone was presented), similar to findings from the previous experiment in which the pressure was self-induced. Importantly, Gray also showed that *movement coordination* was affected by the pressure. In particular, he looked at the variability in the time ratio of the windup (i.e., the time when the batter's lead foot is in the air) and the swing phase (i.e., the time from initiation of the bat swing to minimum bat height). When performance is consistent and at a high level, and the movement is controlled automatically, variability in this ratio is low. However, with the additional pressure created by the prospect of winning extra money, variability in the movement pattern increased significantly. This nicely shows how the regression to a more conscious type of control—induced by pressure to perform well—degrades the fluidity of the motion and makes the outcome less reliable.

Anxiety can have effects on motor coordination similar to those from pressure to perform well. Studies have shown that situations that cause anxiety lead to less fluent and efficient movement patterns; this is also reminiscent of coordination patterns that are seen early in the learning process (e.g., Beuter & Duda, 1985; Weinberg, 1978; Weinberg & Hunt, 1976). In a recent study that used a climbing task, different degrees of anxiety were induced by having participants traverse a wall at two different heights (Pijpers, Oudejans, & Bakker, 2005). Even though the two traverses were identical in terms of the holds for the climber's hands and feet, the higher traverse clearly induced more anxiety (as measured by an anxiety questionnaire and heart rate). As a result, participants performed more exploratory movements (in which a hold was touched without being used as support), maintained longer contact with the holds, and moved more slowly between holds, increasing the total climbing time. Thus, the fear of falling created by the greater height seemed to result in more hesitant behavior and more conscious, step-by-step control.

ATTENTIONAL INSIGHTS

Gary Leffew is a former rodeo bull rider, actor, writer, and stunt coordinator. In 1970 he won the world championship bull-riding competition. He now teaches bull riding at his ranch in California.

On April 18, 2005, KNPR (Nevada Public Radio) aired an interview with Gary Leffew on *Fresh Air*. In this interview, Leffew shared some interesting experiences he had had during his bull-riding career. In particular, he talked about how "negative" thoughts can interfere with performance and how he managed to reverse the vicious cycle of worrying and performance decrements. Interestingly, Leffew also noticed that conscious control attempts were too slow and that they resulted in less than optimal performance (which can be particularly dangerous in bull riding).

Leffew: *Once I got really good at riding . . . I learned to drop . . . out of the conscious level of thinking and get down to the lower levels of thinking, where everything happens much faster and much quicker . . . and, also, when you get down to the lower level, you are kind of at the same level where the animal thinks, and you are able to kind of pick up his thought pattern, where you know where he is going as he is going there, and you . . . become one with him, and you flow with him. It's kind of a Zen-like thing, but it really works.*

Interviewer: *You said earlier that when you started really concentrating on doing well . . . you did worse. How did you get into a different mind-set for this?*

Leffew: *Well, the reason I was doing worse . . . without knowing how the mind works . . . I was worrying a lot. Whenever you worry, you take an end result, a negative end result, and . . . you run it repetitiously through your mind, so much that the mind thinks it's real, and it also thinks that that is what you want to happen. So, you can be in the middle of the best ride you ever started, and all of a sudden self-sabotage takes over and takes you right out of the game. And that was happening over and over again, and I couldn't understand why. I would get started, but I couldn't finish. And then when I started to learn what self-sabotage was and how the mind works, then I learned to reverse the worry process. I started to*

> *worry about how good it would feel to be in perfect time with a great bull . . . what the sound of the crowd would sound like . . . that adrenaline rush of being 15 feet off the ground in complete control of something that out of control. . . . You start to see it differently in your mind, and you keep rehearsing it, and pretty soon it becomes real.*

Interviewer: *It sounds almost as if, when you are on this . . . ton of angry bull, in one of the most scary, intense situations anybody could face, you are actually relaxing.*

Leffew: *You are very relaxed. When you are doing it right, it is the most euphoric experience that you . . . can imagine. Because this bull is so out of control and so powerful, yet you are at one with him. You are just totally at one, and it's an incredible ride. . . .*

Leffew: *I have been throwed (sic) into fences, I have been throwed (sic) over fences . . . the worst thing is when you hit the ground and that ton of animal comes down on you and steps on you.*

Interviewer: *That must yank you out of that Zen state pretty quickly.*

Leffew: *Oh, yeah, but you find that when you are in that Zen state . . . it doesn't happen very often. Every time that I look back . . . and a wreck happened . . . I was in a conscious thought process.*

INSTRUCTION AND FEEDBACK

Thus, stressful situations tend to make people focus more on the actual execution of the skill. However, there could be other reasons why an individual directs more attention than usual to his or her performance. For example, a tennis player might be asked by a less experienced player what exactly she does to produce a certain type of spin. A simple question like this might cause the skilled player to direct more attention to how she coordinates her movements—with the result that the stroke she usually performs flawlessly is suddenly impaired. Or a golfer practicing with a coach might be told to focus on a certain aspect of his technique such as his hip motion. Even instructions like this that are given with the intention of improving performance can, at least temporarily, have a negative effect on performance.

A study by Bob Gray (2004) nicely demonstrates how directing experts' attention to an aspect of the skill affects their performance. Gray looked at the effects of directing attention to either an aspect of skill execution or an unrelated (secondary) task in baseball players. Specifically, Gray had recreational baseball players with less than five years of experience (novices) and expert players with 12 to 19 years of batting experience perform a task that simulated baseball batting. In one condition, the so-called *extraneous* dual-task condition, either a high-pitch or low-pitch tone was presented while participants were batting. Their task was to respond as quickly as possible by saying either "high" or "low." In another condition, the so-called *skill-focused* dual-task condition, participants were also presented with a tone. In this, case, however, they had to indicate whether their bat was moving upward or downward at the moment the tone occurred by saying either "up" or "down." Gray found that temporal errors on the batting task under the extraneous and skill-focused dual-task conditions depended on the level of expertise (see figure 1.2). While novices had smaller errors when they focused on batting (skill-focused condition) than when they performed an unrelated task (extraneous task condition), the opposite was true for experts. Also, in relation to performance without an additional task (single-task condition), experts showed a performance decrement when they focused on the skill, but not when they focused on the extraneous task. Thus, experts' performance was unhampered when they directed their attention to something unrelated to the skill itself. Because experts' skill execution is automated, they have enough spare attentional capacity to attend to other things. Yet, interestingly, asking them to direct their attention to their performance (i.e., whether the bat was moving upward or downward) actually affected their performance negatively.

Similar effects have been found in studies on golf putting and dribbling in soccer (Beilock et al., 2004, 2002; Ford, Hodges, & Williams, 2005). In one golf study (Beilock et al., 2004), expert golfers putted golf balls under a dual-task condition, which required them to detect a target tone (and say "tone" when it was presented), and under a skill-focused condition, in which they had to focus on a straight club motion (and say "straight" when they contacted the ball). The results showed that the experienced golfers were less accurate when they focused on the golf club motion (skill-focused condition) than when they focused on the tone (dual-task condition). This finding is similar to that of Castaneda and Gray (in press), who observed that expert baseball players had larger errors on a batting simulation

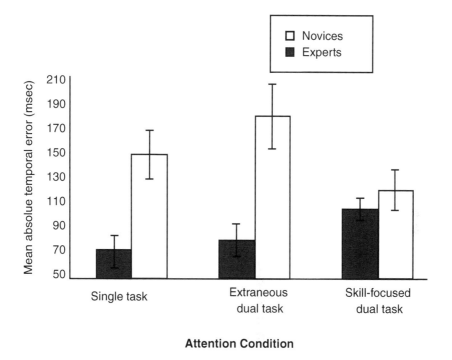

FIGURE 1.2 Batting performance (absolute temporal error) of expert and novice baseball players in the three attention conditions used in the study by Gray (2004). Filled bars: experts; open bars: novices.

Reprinted, by permission, from R. Gray, 2004, "Attending to the execution of a complex sensorimotor skill: Expertise differences, choking, and slumps," *Journal of Experimental Psychology: Applied* 10: 42-54.

task when their attention was directed to their batting performance (hands or bat) as opposed to something not directly related to the action itself (ball trajectory or pitch of a tone). Interestingly, the skill-focused condition in the study by Beilock and colleagues (2004) also resulted in a performance decrement when compared to a single-task condition without a secondary task (which is in line with Gray's [2004] findings). Thus, these findings clearly show that if experienced individuals direct their attention to the details of skill execution, the result is almost certainly a decrement in performance.

While the level of expertise typically differs *between* individuals as a function of their experience with a certain task, the degree of expertise can also differ *within* an individual when the skill is to be executed with different sides of the body. Many sport skills, including basketball shots, soccer kicks, kayak rolls, and parallel turns in skiing, should ideally be performed equally well with the right and left side. Yet, with few exceptions, people typically have a preferred or dominant side, and their performance is better on that side. Would differential attentional focus effects also be found within (experienced) individuals when they were required to perform a skill with their dominant versus nondominant side? Beilock and colleagues (2002) examined this issue by using a soccer dribbling task. Participants had to dribble a soccer ball through a slalom course consisting of several cones, using either their right (dominant) or left (nondominant) foot. In the skill-focused condition, they were required to direct their attention to the side of the foot that was contacting the ball and to indicate whether the inside or outside of their foot was touching the ball when a tone was presented. In the dual-task condition, participants had to listen to a list of words and repeat out loud a target word when it was presented. The experienced soccer players performed better under the dual-task than under the skill-focus condition—provided they used their dominant foot. Interestingly, when they had to use their nondominant left foot, their performance was more effective under the skill-focus than under the dual-task condition. Thus, it appears that skill execution with the less-practiced side reflects execution in an earlier stage of learning—which requires more attentional resources and which suffers when attention is directed elsewhere.

One might argue that in the experiments reviewed (Beilock et al., 2002, 2004; Ford, Hodges, & Williams, 2005; Gray, 2004), the conditions under which the participants performed were somewhat "artificial," in that participants had to say a specific word out loud as soon as a tone was presented or at a certain time during their performance (e.g., when the golf club made contact with the ball). Perhaps waiting for the tone created some sort of interference that is normally not present. Also, requirements such as indicating the direction of the bat at the time of the tone (Gray, 2004) might have altered the performers' visual focus. It might have prompted them to look at the bat and perhaps to slow down the movement to facilitate recognition of bat direction, which is not something baseball players normally do. Therefore, one might ask whether it is indeed the focus on skill execution per se that is detrimental to performance or the interference caused by the additional task requirements.

A study conducted in our laboratory several years ago, however, seems to support the idea that it is the attention directed to the execution of one's movements that is disruptive (Wulf & Weigelt, 1997). In that study, participants practiced the complex ski simulator task that was described earlier for novices (see photo on p. 9). We gave participants four days of practice without any instructions as to how to best perform this task. Nevertheless, they made considerable progress and increased their movement amplitudes from day to day. In the middle of the fourth day, we gave participants instructions about the *optimal* movement pattern by telling them how experts perform this task. Previous studies (e.g., Vereijken, 1991; Vereijken, Whiting, & Beek, 1992; Whiting & Vereijken, 1993; Whiting, Vogt, & Vereijken, 1992) had shown that expert performers take advantage of the energy stored in the stretched rubber belts by letting the rubber belts pull them back until about the middle of the apparatus. Only at this point do they apply force by pushing the platform to the other side. Thus, we asked our participants to try to exert force on the platform after it had passed the center. Obviously, one would expect this "tip" to enhance their performance. This was not what happened, however (see figure 1.3)! On the contrary, performance deteriorated.

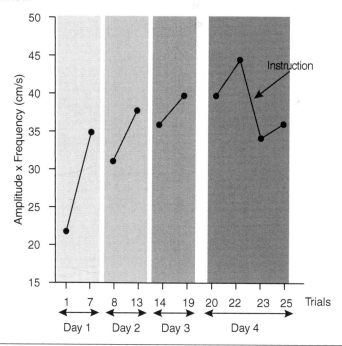

FIGURE 1.3 Overall performance (amplitude × frequency) on the first and last trial on each of three training days (Trials 1, 7, 8, 13, 14, and 19), on the first and last retention trial (Trials 20 and 22), and on the first and last trial with timing-of-forcing instructions (Trials 23 and 25) in the ski simulator study with advanced performers (Wulf & Weigelt, 1997, Experiment 2).

Reprinted with permission, from *Research Quarterly for Exercise and Sport,* Vol. 68, pgs. 362-367, Copyright 1999 by the American Alliance for Health, Physical Education, Recreation and Dance, 1900 Association Drive, Reston, VA 20191.

When participants were given the instruction about the optimal technique, their performance was degraded. Figure 1.4 shows, for four representative individuals, the platform movements on the last trial before the instructions were given and on the first trials after the instructions were given. Without exception, participants' movements became less fluent, jerkier, and slower, and movement amplitudes were smaller. Even though participants recovered somewhat over the next few 90 s trials, at the end of Day 4 their performance had clearly not returned to the level they had reached before they were given the instructions. Thus, even though one might have expected the instructions to have led to an *improvement* in performance, as they referred to the most effective technique, performance actually suffered. At the least, the information did not have an immediate benefit. While it is possible that individuals would have shown performance gains after a longer practice period with the "new" technique, it is clear that there was a performance decrement (at least temporarily) when performers were instructed to direct their attention to a certain aspect of the movement pattern.

More recently, Vuillerme and Nafati (in press) used a task at which we are all experts (perhaps with the exception of young children and those with motor impairments)—standing still on a solid surface—and looked at how directing attention to the task affected the amount of postural sway. They asked their participants, who were young, healthy adults, to stand on a force plate under two conditions (with half of the participants starting with one or the other condition): without any further instructions regarding their attentional focus ("control condition") or with the instruction to deliberately focus on their body sway and to actively control their postural sway ("attention condition"). Vuillerme and Nafati found that, when individuals were consciously trying to reduce their body sway, they actually produced *more* sway than they did under normal (control) conditions. Specifically, the difference between the center of foot pressure and the center of gravity showed more variability under the attention than under the control condition. This measure is seen as an indication of the amount of neuromuscular activity of the leg muscles controlling posture (e.g., Rougier, 2003). In other words, when participants were asked to reduce their sway, they expended more energy and their sway actually increased! This nicely demonstrates how our attempts to consciously control our movements interfere with automatic processes that normally regulate those movements very effectively in highly practiced skills.

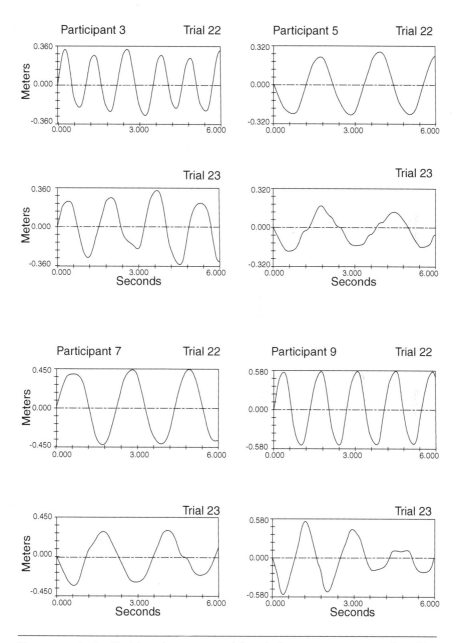

FIGURE 1.4 Position–time curves of the platform movements produced by four representative advanced performers on the last trial without instructions (Trial 22) and on the first trial with instructions (Trial 23) (Wulf & Weigelt, 1997, Experiment 2).

Even if people are not specifically asked to attend to their performance, they might do so spontaneously if given enough time. This
was shown in a golf putting study (Beilock et al., 2004), in which
experts and novices either were allowed to take as much time as
they needed or had to perform under time pressure, that is, within
3 s after they took their stance. The experts performed better under
time pressure than they did when they could take their time. In
contrast, novice golfers putted more accurately when they were not
under time pressure. These findings are in line with the view that
"thinking too much" about the movement is detrimental for expert
performers. Preventing them from doing so actually enhanced their
performance in this study.

These findings raise the question whether the detrimental effects
on performance caused by pressure, anxiety, or simply instructions
aimed at improving performance, can be reduced or even prevented.
The approach discussed in the remaining chapters of this book offers
a potential solution to this problem. First, however, let's take a look
at the effectiveness of other methods that have been proposed as a
means to prevent choking.

ADJUSTING ATTENTIONAL FOCUS

Are there things that skilled performers can do to prevent, or at least
reduce, the risk of choking? Clearly, choking is highly undesirable,
especially when much is at stake, as when the goal is to win a tennis
tournament, get a contract as a result of a musical audition, or save
one's own life or those of others in a dangerous situation. Is there a
way to prevent choking under pressure? Is it possible to design training in such a way that it "inoculates" the individual against choking?
Some scientists have argued that one way to make people immune
to the negative effects of pressure is to have them practice in a situation that promotes self-consciousness (Beilock & Carr, 2001; Lewis
& Linder, 1997). The argument is that, if individuals are used to performing with attention directed to their performance, the self-focused
attention created by situations that induce pressure to perform well
should not be disruptive. Beilock and Carr (2001) attempted to test
this hypothesis by having one group of learners ("self-conscious"
group) practice while being videotaped. Participants were told that
golf teachers and coaches would view the videotapes "to gain a better
understanding of how individuals learn a golf putting skill" (p. 716).
A "high-pressure" posttest was created by informing participants that
they could win $5 if they were able to improve their performance

shown at the end of the practice phase by 20%. Compared to learners who did not receive "self-consciousness" training ("single-task" group) and learners who practiced with a distracting secondary task ("distraction" group), participants tended to show an improvement on the high-pressure test. In contrast, the single-task and distraction groups demonstrated a performance decrement, or choking.

Wan and Huon (2005) replicated this study with a music-related task. Novice musicians were first taught basic note and rhythm reading skills. Then they practiced a keyboard task under one of three conditions: single task, dual task (listening to another piece of music with a different tempo), and video monitoring (being videotaped and instructed to "pay close attention to what you are doing" [p. 161]). In a "high-pressure" test situation that was similar to the one used by Beilock and Carr (2001), the video-monitoring group again showed a performance advantage compared to the other two groups.

Even though these findings seem to suggest that being used to performing under conditions of self-focused attention has an inoculating effect, it is unclear how exactly this type of training would prevent choking. Do individuals still focus on skill execution under pressure? If

With appropriate focus, musicians can use arousal positively and avoid the performance decrements associated with stage fright.

Courtesy of Adina Mornell and Detlef Levin

so, why does this not affect their performance negatively? Or do they eventually stop focusing on their performance for some reason? One possible explanation for these results could be that the test conditions were simply more similar to the conditions under which participants in the "self-conscious" group practiced, as compared to those for participants in the other groups. (Alternatively, if the test condition had required participants to perform under distracting conditions, the "distraction" group participants might have shown an advantage, because they were more used to that particular condition.) It is also possible that, rather than making performers immune to choking, videotaping participants might have increased their motivation to perform well. For example, participants might have set their goals at a higher level. Goal setting has been shown to benefit the performance and learning of motor skills (e.g., Boyce, 1992; Burton, 1994; Kyllo & Landers, 1995; Weinberg, 1994). Thus, whether "self-consciousness training" is indeed effective in preventing choking remains to be seen. In fact, Liao and Master (2002) showed that self-consciousness training in basketball free-throw shooting resulted in poorer performance under pressure than that of a control group. They concluded that "the negative effect of stress on performance is likely to be magnified if a skill is acquired under self-focused attention" (p. 300).

Are there other ways to prevent performance decrements that result from pressure, anxiety, or other factors that induce self-focused attention? What should experts direct their attention to, if anything? Gray (2004) argued that unless we understand "why a self-focused attentional orientation degrades performance in experts . . . a coach can do little more than instruct an athlete facing a high-pressure situation to 'stop thinking about it and just do it'" (p. 52). As we will see in the following chapters, even the performance of experts can benefit when their attention is directed in certain ways. While it remains to be seen whether choking in pressure situations can be prevented in this way, there is at least evidence that their performance, in general, can be improved through attention focusing.

SUMMARY

As we have seen, many changes occur when we practice a motor skill. One of the most prevalent changes is a reduction in the amount of attention we need to direct to the execution of the skill. Because of this, experienced individuals are usually able to direct their attention to other aspects of their performance, or even to unrelated things, without suffering a decrement in performance. However, if their attention is directed to the details of their action, their performance is typically affected negatively. Many scientists believe that beginners, in contrast to experts, need to pay attention to those details in order to facilitate the learning process (e.g., Beilock & Carr, 2001, 2004). The underlying assumption is that there is no way around the first cognitive stage and that, eventually, movement execution will become automatic as a "natural" consequence of extensive practice. Other scientists have different views. They believe that in order to speed up automatization (and to reduce the likelihood of performance breakdowns in stressful situations), movements should be executed "as if they were automatic" from the beginning, or at least as early as possible. While some argue that "thinking" about the coordination of the movement should occur before and after, but not during, the execution of the skill (e.g., Singer, 1985, 1988), others contend that thought processes are generally harmful and should be avoided altogether (e.g., Masters, 1992, 2000; Masters, Polman, & Hammond, 1993).

Anybody who has ever tried to learn a complex motor skill knows that is basically impossible either to attend to all of aspects of performance or to "just do it." That beginners somehow need to focus on the skill seems to make sense. Yet there are usually a multitude of things that one could direct one's attention to. A novice golfer could direct his attention, for example, to the grip, his wrist or hip motion, the club head, the anticipated trajectory of the ball, or the hole. A surfer might pay attention to the pressure exerted by each foot, her posture, the tilt of the surfboard, or the waves. What should a learner focus on? What should coaches or instructors direct a learner's attention to in order to facilitate learning? Do certain attentional foci work better than others? Similar questions can be asked for more advanced, or even expert, performers. Can their performance be optimized if their attention is directed to certain aspects of the task rather than others? This might be especially relevant for performers who have a flaw in their technique that needs to be corrected. Of course, if choking under pressure could be reduced or even prevented through the use of simple attention focusing strategies, many disappointments might be avoided.

In the following chapters, we will consider how the performance and learning of motor skills can be improved through the use of instructions and feedback that direct the individual's focus of attention to the movement *effect*. The effectiveness of this approach has been demonstrated for a variety of skills, as well as skill levels, and the findings have important implications for practical settings.

PRACTICAL APPLICATIONS

ATTENTIONAL CAPACITY

As the learning of a motor skill progresses, less and less attention is required for the control of the action. Thus, more attentional capacity can be dedicated to other aspects of the task (or unrelated things).

- How does this apply to your sport?
- What advantage does the availability of spare attentional capacity have for a ball player, gymnast or dancer, skier, sailor, or musician?
- Why would it be important for individuals with motor impairments to attain at least a certain degree of automaticity, for example in walking or speech production?

PERFORMANCE UNDER PRESSURE

When skilled performers consciously attend to the details of their actions, the result is typically that the fluidity of their movements is disrupted and performance is degraded.

- Under what circumstance does this usually occur, and what are the reasons for this?
- How can "self-focused" attention, or the detrimental effects of it, be prevented?
- If you were a golfer in a situation in which much was at stake, what would you focus on?
- What could a basketball coach instruct her players to focus on during free-throw shooting, especially when under pressure?

INSTRUCTIONS FOR NOVICES

Giving novices, or unskilled performers, instructions about the correct movement pattern is not always beneficial. This is disconcerting, considering the ubiquity of instructions in training settings.

- What could be the reason for the fact that instructions are sometimes ineffective, or even detrimental to learning?
- How can a teacher or coach give instructions that facilitate the learning process instead of hindering it?
- What would you instruct a novice skier or windsurfer to focus on when turning?
- What could a physical therapist instruct a Parkinson's patient to direct attention to while practicing balance on an unstable surface?
- What should novice juggler focus on?

FUTURE DIRECTIONS

Research on the effects of attention focusing instructions at different stages of learning has yielded important insights into the attentional demands of performance at different levels of expertise. Yet, in some of those studies, the different conditions under which participants performed were not counterbalanced, leaving the possibility that order (or practice) effects might have influenced the results. Counterbalancing procedures, in which each of three conditions, for example, is performed first, second, or last by different participants, would be important in future studies. Also, most studies have looked only at *performance* effects rather than *learning* effects of different attentional foci during practice. To determine how different attentional foci affect the learning of motor skills, it is necessary to include retention or transfer testing (see chapter 2 for an explanation of the performance–learning distinction and the concept of retention and transfer tests). In short, learning studies require different groups of participants, each practicing under different attentional focus conditions (rather than performing under all conditions), who are later tested under identical conditions—or on a level playing field—in a retention or transfer test. Future studies should include those tests.

"Choking under pressure" is a phenomenon that clearly warrants more research. While scientists have a fairly good understanding of its underlying causes, we still don't have good methods to prevent it. Future studies should examine the effectiveness of different attentional focus strategies that athletes, musicians, or motorically challenged individuals (e.g., persons after stroke), for example, could use in stressful situations. Those studies should use "fair" test conditions (i.e., conditions that are not more similar to certain practice conditions than others) and preferably those that have practical validity.

A windsurfer may find their attention drawn to the water, the wind, their body, or their surfboard.

CHAPTER 2

INTERNAL VERSUS EXTERNAL FOCUS INSTRUCTIONS

I magine a windsurfer who is trying to learn a "power jibe." This maneuver requires the well-timed coordination of leg and arm movements and appropriate weight shifts during its various phases, coupled with the precise timing of flipping the sail. In addition, windsurfers often have to deal with threats to their balance due to choppy water or gusty wind. To learn the power jibe, our windsurfer buys a magazine in which the proper technique is described. The description is illustrated with a sequence of photos showing the step-by-step execution of the jibe. With the photos providing a clear and detailed image of the movement sequence, and the verbal description highlighting the important points of each phase of the jibe, this might seem like a good way to learn.

However, after repeatedly studying the sequence of movements, going through it mentally, and practicing it physically on the water, the windsurfer finds that the result is clearly not what she had hoped for. Little, if any, progress is to be seen even after several hours of practice. Frustrated about this lack of success, she decides not to concentrate on the coordination of her body movements anymore. Instead, she decides to simply focus on the board, trying to ensure that it turns as planned. The result of this change in attentional focus is amazing: The jibes are much faster, more fluent—and much more successful!

Such a dramatic performance improvement, resulting from a simple shift in the focus of attention, might seem hard to believe. Yet this is exactly the experience

I had when I windsurfed on Lake Garda, Italy, in 1996. Focusing on my body movements and consciously trying to control them was clearly not very effective. In contrast, when I focused my attention on the *effect* that I was trying to achieve with these movements, namely the effects of my movements on the surfboard, my performance was suddenly much better. This experience was most impressive!

At the same time, I wondered whether this attentional strategy worked only for me or whether it was generally an effective strategy. In other words, would other people also benefit from directing their attention to the movement effect rather than the movements themselves? For researchers, there is only one way to find out, and that is to do an experimental study.

Let's take a look at the experimental evidence for how different attentional foci affect the performance and learning of motor skills. Specifically, we will look at studies that compared the effectiveness of instructions directing learners' attention to the effects of their movements with that of instructions directing attention to the movements themselves. Whereas the first studies to address this issue used laboratory tasks, including relatively challenging balance tasks, several studies that followed up on those first experiments used sport skills to determine whether the findings were generalizable to real-life skills. It also turned out that the "distance" of the movement effect that an individual focuses on seems to have an influence on his or her performance. These studies are reviewed next. In addition, we will address two important questions: Are there individual differences in how effective different types of attentional foci are? And: Does a performer's focus of attention have only a temporary influence on her or his *performance,* or can it actually affect how well a skill is *learned*?

FIRST EXPERIMENTAL EVIDENCE

Inspired by my windsurfing experience, my student Markus Höβ at the Technical University of Munich and I decided to do an experiment to examine whether the type of attentional focus can indeed affect the learning of motor skills. We used the ski simulator for this study. The instructions we gave participants were similar to the instructions we had used in our previous study, discussed in chapter 1. However, instead of telling participants when to push the platform, the instructions referred to *how* to push the platform. This change was based on the findings from another experiment, in which we observed that experienced performers exert force on the platform with the *outer* foot. That is, when the platform moves to the right, they push the platform with the right foot, and when it moves to the left they push with the left foot. Therefore, we instructed one group of performers to try to push the platform with the outer foot and focus on that foot. We labeled this type of attentional focus "internal," as it referred to the performers' body movements (i.e., the movements of their feet). We instructed another group of participants to focus on the force they exerted on the *wheels* of the platform. We call a focus that is directed at the effect of one's movement on the environment, such as the wheels (or an apparatus or implement), an "external" focus. If you look at the photo on page 9 again, you will notice that the wheels are directly under the performer's feet. Thus, the difference in the instructions, and in the focus of attention induced by them, was minimal. Yet one group of participants directed their attention to their own movements (internal focus), whereas the other group focused on the effects of their movements on the "environment," or apparatus (external focus).

We reasoned that if such a small difference in the attentional focus indeed has an influence on how well people learn a motor skill, this effect, if any, has to be quite powerful. In addition to the internal and external focus groups, we had a control group that was not given any attentional focus instructions. We added this group to see whether an external focus would actually *enhance* learning, or whether an internal focus would be *detrimental* to learning, compared to when people were left to their own devices and were free to explore the optimal technique.

All participants in our study practiced the ski simulator task for eight 90 s trials on each of two consecutive days. On the very first trial, all three groups were similar in performance and produced amplitudes of about 20 cm (8 in.) to either side. (The maximum amplitude to either side is about 50 cm [20 in.].) However, the performance improvements across practice were quite different for the three groups. The external focus group showed a greater improvement than the other two groups. At the end of the second day, the external group had average amplitudes of 47 cm, whereas the internal group and control group had amplitudes of 35 and 41 cm, respectively (see figure 2.1).

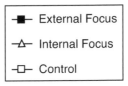

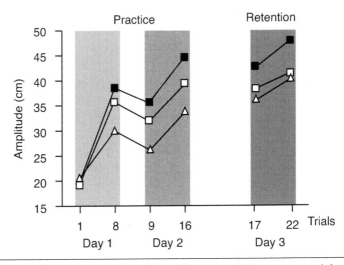

FIGURE 2.1 Average amplitudes of the internal focus, external focus, and control groups on the ski simulator (Wulf, Höβ, & Prinz, 1998, Experiment 1).

Reprinted, by permission, from G. Wulf, M. Höβ, and W. Prinz, 1998, "Instructions for motor learning: Differential effects of internal versus external focus of attention," *Journal of Motor Behavior* 30: 169-179.

Researchers in motor skill learning, however, are interested not only in the immediate changes in performance when individuals practice a task under certain conditions. What is even more interesting is how groups that practice under different conditions—in this case, different attentional focus conditions—perform after a certain interval and when they are not given any instructions or reminders. Learning is typically defined as a *relatively permanent* change in a person's capability to perform a certain skill (e.g., Schmidt & Lee, 2005). Therefore, researchers use so-called retention tests that are performed after an interval of at least one day, but sometimes several days or even weeks. The purpose of this interval is to give any temporary effects of the various practice conditions (caused, for example, by different degrees of fatigue or motivation) a chance to dissipate—leaving only the relatively permanent, or learning, effects. Thus, retention tests are used to determine which practice condition was most conducive to learning.

An important aspect of these tests, aside from the interval after which they are conducted, is that all groups perform under the same conditions (in this case, *without* attentional focus instructions). Only then can the performance of different groups be compared directly, so that researchers can draw conclusions about the effectiveness of different practice conditions for learning.

In our ski simulator study, participants performed a retention test one day after the end of practice. We did not give them any attentional focus instructions that day. Participants were simply told to perform the ski simulator task again for another six trials. Almost to our surprise, the retention results were again very clear: Participants who had adopted an external focus during practice produced, on average, 47 cm amplitudes, whereas those with an internal focus or no focus instructions (control group) produced amplitudes of 40 and 41 cm, respectively. Thus, the external focus instructions indeed resulted in more effective learning than did the internal focus instructions or no instructions.

Even though the internal focus instructions were not detrimental relative to the no-instruction control condition in this case, as they were in the ski simulator study that Cornelia Weigelt and I (Wulf & Weigelt, 1997) had done earlier (presumably because of the slightly different nature of the instructions; see section "Novice Motor Learning and Performance"), they were no more effective than no instructions at all. Essentially, the "tip" about how to perform the task more efficiently was useless if it was worded in a way that directed participants' attention to their own movements. How is this possible? Perhaps the potential benefits of knowing how to perform the skill were canceled out by the detrimental effects of directing attention to their movement coordination. This might also explain why there were no significant differences between the internal focus and control groups in this study (as well as in other studies we will discuss later). Importantly, these findings demonstrate nicely how the negative effects of self-focused attention can be avoided, and how performance can be *improved*—namely, through directing attention away from the execution of the movement and to the movement's effects on the environment.

Obviously, we were excited about these results. Yet when we first tried to publish this study, the reviewers were skeptical. Admittedly, it was hard to believe that such a small difference in the focus of attention could have such a strong influence on performance and learning. Among those reviewers of the manuscript was a friend and colleague from Texas A&M University, Professor Charles Shea. To our disappointment, he asked us to try to replicate the findings with another task before he would be able to recommend the study for publication. (Charlie is still a friend, though!) In fact, as it turned out, Charlie was instrumental in conducting the follow-up study. I spent some time in Charlie's laboratory a few weeks later, and we both thought about a task that might be used for a second study. Eventually we found a stabilometer in a storage room that looked as though it hadn't been used in years. We decided to use it. The stabilometer task is a dynamic balance task that basically requires the coordination of the whole body (see photo).

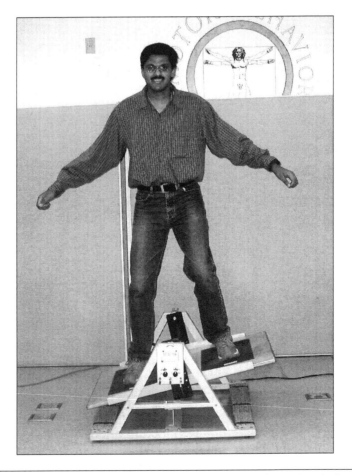

Participant balancing on the stabilometer. The goal is to keep the platform in a horizontal position.

In order to determine whether an external focus would result in better balance than an internal focus, we compared two groups. One group of participants was instructed to focus on keeping their feet horizontal, while another group was instructed to focus on keeping two little markers horizontal (these were attached to the platform in front of their feet; see photo on page 40). The first group (feet) was our internal focus group; the second one (markers) was our external focus group. It should be pointed out that participants did not look at their feet or the markers, respectively. Rather, we asked them to look straight ahead, but to concentrate on their feet or the markers. (In all attentional focus experiments, we try to make sure that visual information is not confounded with the instructed focus of attention. This way, we can be sure that performance differences between groups, if any, are not due to the fact that participants *look* at different things, but rather to what they concentrate on.) Participants practiced on two days, with seven 90 s trials per day, and we gave them reminders regarding their focus of attention before each trial.

Not surprisingly, both groups improved their performance; that is, their average deviations of the platform from the horizontal became smaller across practice (see figure 2.2). Interestingly, even though there were basically no performance differences between the two groups during the first two days, the external focus group demonstrated significantly better balance on a retention test on Day 3. That is, despite the minimal difference in the actual locus of attention (the tips of the feet actually touched the markers), focusing on the movement effect (i.e., the markers) was more effective for learning than focusing on movements of the feet. Thus, we were able to replicate the external focus benefits first shown with the ski simulator task—and the study was finally published.

In light of these findings, it is interesting to look back at other studies and to see that similar effects have actually been reported earlier, although not in the context of "internal" versus "external" foci of attention. The results of a study by Roy Baumeister (1984), a professor of social psychology, are nicely in line with ours. Baumeister used a commercially available "roll-up" game that consists of two rods attached to a vertical board and a metal ball resting on the rods. The task of the person holding the ends of the rods is to move the rods horizontally in such a way that the ball rolls up an incline and drops into the hole that is farthest from the starting point. Baumeister found that participants who were instructed to be aware of their hands while performing the task performed

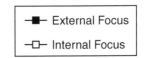

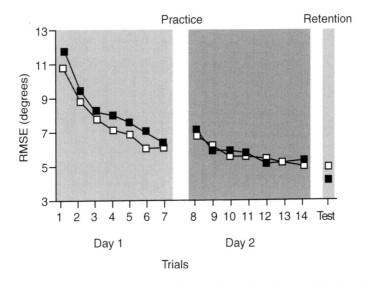

FIGURE 2.2 Deviations of the stabilometer platform from the horizontal (root-mean-square error) for the internal focus and external focus groups (Wulf, Höβ, & Prinz, 1998, Experiment 2).

Reprinted, by permission, from G. Wulf, M. Höβ, and W. Prinz, 1998, "Instructions for motor learning: Differential effects of internal versus external focus of attention," *Journal of Motor Behavior* 30: 169-179.

more poorly than participants who were given similar instructions regarding the ball.

While it was nice to see that the learning of two relatively difficult balance tasks benefited from external focus instructions, as well as to see previous findings in agreement with those results, the next question was obvious: Would the learning of "real-life" skills, such as sport skills, also be enhanced if people adopted an external compared to an internal focus?

SPORT SKILL LEARNING

As you will remember, the first indication that adopting an external focus might be more effective than an internal focus came from my windsurfing experience. This seemed to suggest that an external focus might be beneficial for sport skills as well. However, scientists prefer to have experimental evidence before they accept that a given phenomenon is "real." Therefore, we decided to do an experiment with a real-life skill: hitting golf balls. This experiment is described next. Since then, my colleagues and I, as well as other researchers, have followed up on previous studies and have examined attentional focus effects on the learning of other sport skills, including basketball, soccer, jumping, and tennis skills. Some of these are discussed in the subsequent sections.

GOLF

In our third study, we asked participants, who had no experience with golf, to practice pitch shots (Wulf, Lauterbach, & Toole, 1999). We first gave them basic instructions and demonstrations regarding the stance, grip, and posture. They were also allowed to swing the club (without hitting a ball), and the experimenter gave them feedback about their technique. After this initial phase, which lasted about 10 min, we gave two groups of participants slightly different attentional focus instructions: We asked one group to focus particularly on the swing of their arms and another group to focus on the swing of the club. Thus, all participants were basically given the same information about the technique; the only difference was that one set of instructions induced an internal focus (arms), while the other induced an external focus (club).

The target that participants tried to hit was a circle with a diameter of 90 cm (35 in.). It was placed at a distance of 15 m (16.4 yd) from where the participant was standing. Around the target we drew four concentric circles with radii of 1.45 m, 2.45 m, 3.45 m, and 4.45 m. The four zones created by those circles were used to determine the distance from the target. The experimenter recorded 5 points if the ball landed on the target, 4 points if it landed in the zone around the target, 3 points if it landed in the next zone, and so forth. If the ball landed outside the largest zone, 0 points were recorded for that trial.

The results were very clear. From the beginning of the practice phase, the external focus instructions greatly enhanced the accuracy of the shots. Figure 2.3 shows the mean accuracy scores across blocks of 10 trials for participants who practiced with an internal or external focus, respectively. (Remember, higher scores indicate better performance.) While both groups improved their scores

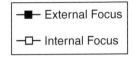

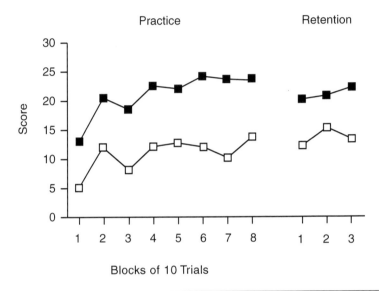

FIGURE 2.3 Average scores achieved by participants who adopted an internal focus (arms) or external focus (club) while practicing golf pitch shots (Wulf, Lauterbach, & Toole, 1999).

Reprinted with permission, from *Research Quarterly for Exercise and Sport,* Vol. 70, pgs. 120-126, Copyright 1999 by the American Alliance for Health, Physical Education, Recreation and Dance, 1900 Association Drive, Reston, VA 20191.

across the 80 practice trials, the external focus group was much more accurate than the internal focus group. Importantly, this was the case not only for practice, when participants were given attentional focus instructions and reminders before each block. Even on a retention test that was performed one day later—and during which no instructions or reminders were given—the external focus group was superior.

Thus, the instructions that directed the learners' attention to the effects of their movements on the implement (golf club) were again more effective for learning than instructions that directed their attention to their movements. These results provided the first experimental evidence that the learning of sport skills can be facilitated if instructions are worded so as to induce an external, rather than internal, focus. Considering that most coaches give instructions that refer to the performer's body movements, these results have important practical implications: A simple change in the wording of instructions can make an enormous difference and actually improve performance!

We recently replicated the golf study with one difference: We added a control group to the internal and external focus conditions (Wulf & Su, in press, Experiment 1). Control group participants were given the same basic instructions as the other two groups, but were not given additional instructions about what they should focus their attention on (as in the ski simulator study discussed earlier). The internal and external focus groups performed similarly to the respective groups in the first golf experiment (see figure 2.4). An external focus again resulted in more effective learning. The control group's performance, in both practice and retention, was similar to

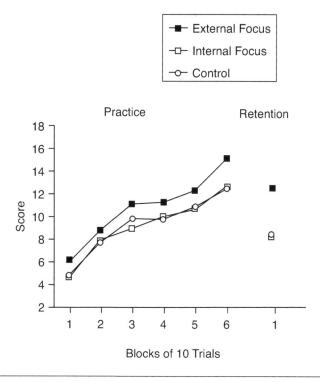

FIGURE 2.4 Average scores achieved by participants who adopted an internal focus or an external focus or received no attentional focus instructions (control group) while practicing golf pitch shots (Wulf & Su, in press).

Adapted from Wulf and Su in press.

that of the internal focus group. This is reminiscent of the ski simulator experiment, in which the internal focus instructions provided no advantage compared to not giving any information. This result supports our conclusion that in order to *enhance* learning, instructions need to induce an external focus of attention.

Another recent study (Perkins-Ceccato, Passmore, & Lee, 2003) appeared to come to a different conclusion, namely, that an internal focus might be more advantageous than an external focus for novice golfers. However, differences between internal and external focus conditions were found only in the trial-to-trial variability in the shots, not in accuracy. Also, the instructions given under the two conditions were somewhat vague, and they directed attention to different aspects of the skill. Specifically, in the internal focus condition, participants were told to "concentrate on the form of the golf swing and to adjust the force of their swing depending on the distance of the shot"; in the external focus condition, they were instructed to "concentrate on hitting the ball as close to the target pylon as possible" (p. 596). While the external focus instructions were relatively unambiguous, one may ask how participants might have interpreted the internal focus instructions. With an emphasis placed on the force of the swing, it is possible that individuals actually focused on the impact that the *club* had on the ball. If so, this would, in fact, constitute an external focus. The performance advantage seen under this condition, compared to the "target" condition, would actually be in line with the results of one of our studies (Wulf et al., 2000), in which a focus on the swing of the club was more effective than a focus on the ball trajectory and the target in novices. (This study is discussed in more detail in chapter 5.) The study by Perkins-Ceccato and colleagues highlights the need to give specific instructions, as well as internal and external focus instructions that are comparable in terms of the information they provide and the aspect of the skill that they direct the performer's attention to.

BASKETBALL

To further examine the generalizability of external focus benefits to sport skills, Tiffany Zachry, one of my graduate students at the University of Nevada, Las Vegas, looked at basketball free throws (Zachry et al., 2005). (Another purpose of the study was to help us understand the reasons for the differential effects of internal versus external foci of attention, but this aspect of the study will be discussed in chapter 4.) That study differed from the studies we have talked about so far in that all participants performed free throws in both an internal and an external focus condition. Whereas in the previous studies, participants performed in a practice phase that involved either internal or external focus instructions and then performed a retention test without instructions so that learning effects could be assessed, Zachry's study was more concerned with the immediate effects of an individual's focus of attention on his or her performance. Thus, all participants were required to perform basketball free throws while focusing either on their wrist motion (internal focus) or the rim of the basket (external focus). The order of attentional focus conditions was counterbalanced between participants; that is, an equal number of participants started with an internal focus and then switched to an external focus, and vice versa. Scores were awarded for the accuracy of the free throws. Specifically, we awarded 5 points if the ball went through the hoop, 3 points for balls touching the hoop, 2 points for balls touching the board and the hoop, and 1 point for balls touching the board. A missed shot was given a score of 0.

These results confirmed previous findings. When participants were instructed to focus their attention on the rim (external focus), their accuracy scores were higher than when they focused on the flexion of their wrist (internal focus): The average accuracy score was 2.6 for the external focus condition and was 2.1 for the internal focus condition. This finding extended the findings of previous studies that used learning paradigms, with different groups practicing under different attentional focus conditions. Zachry's results showed that the type of focus has a relatively strong and immediate effect on performance, and that performance changes as the individual changes their focus. Even though participants had basketball-related experience, their free-throw accuracy was higher when they focused externally rather than internally. This suggests that extended practice periods with the respective attentional focus are not a necessary precondition for those effects to manifest themselves. When performers already have experience with the task, their performance can be affected basically immediately by the attentional focus that they are instructed—or that they decide—to adopt.

In many practical settings, instructors not only give learners instructions about the correct movement pattern, but also use demonstrations to supplement the verbal information. Sometimes teachers or instructors demonstrate the goal movement themselves. For example, a ski instructor might show a novice skier a certain type of turn, or a tennis coach might demonstrate how to hit a ball with topspin. In other situations, videotapes are used to demonstrate the correct technique. This can be particularly useful in cases in which live demonstrations are difficult. For instance, in windsurfing classes, instructors often show videotapes of expert performers (sometimes in slow motion) to give the learner an idea of the movement sequence required for a certain maneuver, such as a water start or a jibe. Also, many people buy videotapes in hopes of improving their golf, tennis, or sailing skills. In the classroom or in other settings in which learners are taught in groups, teachers sometimes have students demonstrate a skill, even if their technique is not perfect, or in order to point out a typical mistake that should be avoided. Thus, observational practice is a commonly used training method when it comes to motor skill learning, and it has indeed been shown to be quite effective (see McCullagh & Weiss, 2001, for a review; e.g., Hebert & Landin, 1994; McCullagh & Meyer, 1997; Shea et al., 2000; Shea, Wulf, & Whitacre, 1999).

Whether demonstrations involve live or video models, or whether the model is an expert or another learner, model presentations are frequently accompanied by verbal instructions that direct the learners' attention to critical aspects of the goal movement pattern. In particular, when the skill to be learned is relatively complex, it is important to facilitate the processing of the information through appropriate instructions. Otherwise, the amount of information provided by the model presentation may be overwhelming for the learner, or the learner may not be aware of what the critical aspects of the skill are (e.g., McCullagh & Weiss, 2001).

Does the focus of attention that is induced by these instructions play a role in this context as well? Can learning be enhanced if the instructions given in combination with model presentations direct learners' attention to the *effects* of the model's or their own movements? It is probably fair to say that in many practical settings, the instructions given in conjunction with model presentations tend to direct the learners' attention to the important aspects of movement coordination. In fact, in many experimental studies in which model presentations were supplemented with instructions or feedback (e.g., Hebert & Landin, 1994; McCullagh & Meyer, 1997; Weeks & Anderson, 2000), one can argue that the information induced an internal focus. Of course, it is possible that the observation of a model is so powerful that it overshadows any effects of the type of focus promoted by concomitantly given instructions. Yet, given the reliability of the external focus advantages that we had seen in other studies, we wanted to examine whether the attentional focus induced by instructions was important in the context of observational practice as well.

In a study that was conducted in collaboration with Judith Parma and Sara Eder in Munich, Germany, we had male and female high school students learn a basketball layup (Wulf, Eder, & Parma, 2005). Even though all the participants had, on occasion, played basketball in physical education classes, none had received formal instructions regarding the layup. All participants performed the layup with their dominant (right) hand. They practiced the layup on two days (12 trials per day), which were separated by three days. At the beginning of each practice day and before every third practice trial, we showed them the video model of an expert performing the layup. Along with each video model presentation we gave them one of three instructions regarding different aspects of the technique. The instructions differed slightly for two different groups, however: They induced either a more internal or a more external focus of attention. The specific instructions are shown in table 2.1.

Four days after the practice phase, participants performed a retention test during which no model presentations were used and no instructions were given. We were interested in how the focus of attention adopted during practice would affect learning in terms of movement outcome (i.e., the accuracy of the shots). Different numbers of points were awarded depending on whether the ball went through the basket or touched the backboard or hoop. The results of that study are shown in figure 2.5. Accuracy scores increased for both internal and external focus groups across the practice phase. Even though the groups did not differ significantly during practice, on the retention test the external focus group participants demonstrated a clear advantage. Their scores were significantly higher than those of participants who had received internal focus instructions with the video presentations.

Another recent study looked at how the type of attentional focus, induced by instructions given in conjunction with video demonstrations, affects the accuracy of basketball free-throw shooting (Al-Abood et al., 2002). In that study, participants watched a video of an expert model performing a basketball free throw. While one group of participants, the "movement dynamics" group, was instructed to pay attention particularly to the model's movement form, another group, the "movement effects" group, was instructed to focus on

TABLE 2.1   BASKETBALL LAYUP INTERNAL AND
EXTERNAL FOCUS INSTRUCTIONS

Task type	Basketball layup[a]	
Goal	Ball through the basket	
Instructions	**Internal focus**	**External focus**
	1. Dribble the ball once when your left foot is on the ground; take two steps and jump off of your left foot.	1. Dribble the ball once, use the two available floor contacts, and jump off of the leg that is farther away from the basket.
	2. Jump straight up and pull up your right knee.	2. Jump toward the ceiling so that you land under the basket and would be able to catch the ball; pull your knee up toward the basket.
	3. Extend your elbow and throw the ball at the red triangle; flip your wrist.	3. Throw the ball at the red triangle when you are closest to the basket; release the ball as if you were waving it "good-bye."

Adapted from Wulf, Eder, and Parma 2005.

[a]The rectangle on the backboard was divided into two halves by a diagonal from the upper left corner to the lower right corner. The right upper half (triangle) was marked red and served as a focal point for participants in both conditions (see instruction 3).

how the model scored a basket. Thus, the instructions were somewhat less specific than those in our basketball study. Also, Al-Abood and colleagues (2002) did not provide participants with physical practice trials between model presentations. Rather, they compared the performances of the two groups on a pretest, conducted before the video demonstrations, to those on a posttest performed after the video presentations. They found that while the movement dynamics group showed no improvement in the accuracy of their shots from pre- to posttest, the movement effects group demonstrated a significant improvement in their scores.

Thus, despite differences in the methods, both studies demonstrate that the type of attentional focus induced by instructions given in

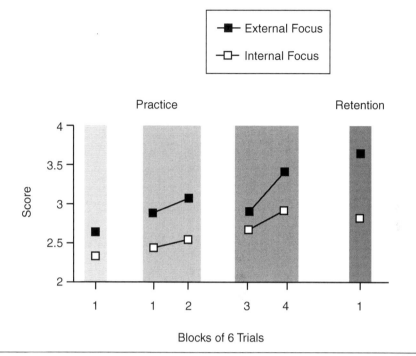

FIGURE 2.5   Accuracy scores of groups adopting an internal or external focus while performing a basketball layup (Wulf, Eder, & Parma, 2005).

combination with model demonstrations has an impact on the performance and learning of the skill: Directing performers' attention away from the coordination of the model's or their own movements (or both) and toward the outcome of the action was more effective than directing attention to the movement pattern. The fact that the influence of the instructions was not canceled out by the typically strong effects of observational practice per se underscores the potency of the attentional focus effect.

DART THROWING

At the University of Hull (United Kingdom), David Marchant did a study for his doctoral dissertation in which he examined attentional focus effects on dart throwing accuracy (Marchant, Clough, & Crawshaw, in press). Specifically, Marchant and colleagues instructed one group of participants (internal focus) to "(1) feel the weight of the dart in their hand; (2) think about drawing the dart back to the ear; (3) feel the bend in the elbow; and (4) feel the dart as it left the fingertips." In contrast, participants in another group (external focus) were instructed to "(1) focus on the centre of the dart board; (2) slowly begin to expand upon perspectives on the dart board; (3) then refocus on the centre of the dart board, expanding the centre, and making it as large as possible; and (4) toss the dart when so focused." A third group (control) was not given any focus instructions. Participants first performed 10 practice throws, during which internal and external focus participants were reminded to use their particular attentional strategy. This was followed by 40 test throws without further instructions. The results showed that, throughout the whole test phase, those individuals who were given external focus instructions were more accurate than those who were given internal focus instructions.

Thus, these results nicely replicate those of the studies described earlier. Yet, in contrast to what happened in other studies that included control groups without attentional focus instructions (e.g., Wulf, Höβ, & Prinz, 1998; Wulf & McNevin, 2003; Wulf & Su, in press; Wulf, Wächter, & Wortmann, 2003), the control group in the Marchant and colleagues (in press) experiment performed as well as the external focus group and more effectively than the internal focus group. This contrasts with findings from the previous studies in which the external focus instructions provided a benefit compared to no instructions (control) or internal focus instructions. There are at least two potential reasons for the fact that control group and external focus participants showed similar proficiencies in this study. One is related to the task, which—as the authors acknowledge—might have promoted an external focus in and of itself, even in the control condition without specific focus instructions. Furthermore, the complexity of the focus instructions might have reduced their effectiveness. This latter issue is discussed in more detail in chapter 4.

FOOTBALL

In her master's thesis, Zachry (2005) found benefits resulting from an external focus for soccer-style American football place kicking (field goal kicking). Zachry recruited participants from our general student population at UNLV who had never kicked a football before. These novices were first given general instructions about the technique as well as a demonstration. Then they performed football field goal-style kicks into a net that was about 5 m (5.5 yd) away. In the center of the net, at a height of 1.9 m (2 yd), was a yellow square (10 by 10 cm [4 by

4 in.]). The goal was to kick the ball so that it hit the square. Everyone performed seven kicks under each of the three following conditions (with the order being counterbalanced among participants): (a) no attentional focus instructions (control condition), (b) focus on the part of the foot that would be contacting the ball (internal focus condition), and (c) focus on the part of the ball that they would be contacting with their foot (external focus condition). The percentage of successful kicks for each condition is shown in figure 2.6. As you can see, individuals were significantly more likely to hit the target when they focused on the ball, as opposed to when they focused on their foot or were not given focus instructions. This nicely demonstrates again that a very small difference in the attentional focus can have a substantial influence on the accuracy of a movement.

SOCCER

Another study, which I did with two collaborators in Germany, Sebastian Wächter and Stefan Wortmann, we used a soccer instep kick to examine the influence of external versus internal focus instructions (Wulf, Wächter, & Wortmann, 2003). Participants were German female

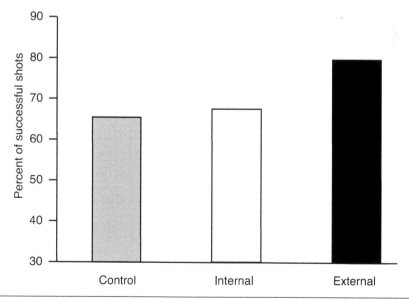

FIGURE 2.6 Percentage of shots made under control, internal focus, and external focus conditions in the study by Zachry (2005).

From T. Zachry, 2005, *Effects of attentional focus on kinematics and muscle activation patterns as a function of expertise.* Masters Thesis. University of Nevada, Las Vegas. By permission of author.

high school students between the ages of 16 and 18 years. Aside from the relatively young age of the participants, a unique feature of this experiment was that participants practiced in groups of five, rather than individually. Thus, the practice situation was more similar to that of typical classroom settings than to a laboratory experiment. Prior to the actual practice phase, all participants were given basic instructions as to the correct technique. In addition, they were shown a series of photographs depicting the sequencing of the instep kick, and the experimenter demonstrated the correct technique twice. To generate specific instructions for the experimental manipulation, we consulted a soccer textbook (Bauer, 2001) and chose four statements that described the critical aspects of the correct technique. The statements were worded in a way that can be assumed to induce an internal focus (see left side of table 2.2). We then "translated" these statements into ones that contained basically the same information but induced more of an external focus (see right side of table 2.2). Before every other practice trial, one of the four statements was given to participants.

TABLE 2.2   SOCCER INTERNAL AND EXTERNAL FOCUS INSTRUCTIONS

Task type	Soccer instep kick	
Goal	Accurately kick soccer ball to rectangular target	
Instructions	**Internal focus**	**External focus**
	1. Make sure the nonkicking foot is positioned next to the ball at a distance of one foot width.	1. Make sure the nonkicking foot is positioned next to the ball at a distance of the width of a goal post.
	2. The kicking foot is fixated in a hyperextended position.	2. The kicking foot is hyperextended like that of a ballerina.
	3. Remember to kick the ball with the instep of your foot.	3. Remember to kick the ball with the laces of your shoe.
	4. The upper body should be bent forward slightly.	4. The upper body should be bent over the nonkicking leg and the ball.

Column A: Reprinted from Women in Sport and Physical Activity Journal Vol. 12, No 1 (2003) with permission from the National Association for Girls and Women in Sport (NAGWS), 1900 Association Drive, Reston, VA 20191-1599.

A rectangular target, with several zones around it, was painted on a foam mat that was placed vertically against a wall. This way we were able to determine the accuracy of the shots. One day after the practice session, which consisted of 30 trials, all participants performed retention and transfer tests without attentional focus instructions. While retention tests are typically used in motor learning studies to assess how well the practiced skill was retained, transfer tests are used to determine the generalizability of what was learned to variations of the practiced skill or to novel situations. In our study, the transfer conditions differed from those in practice and retention, in which participants kicked a stationary ball, in that they were required to kick a moving ball. Balls were rolled down a ramp so that they always approached participants from the same angle (45°) and at the same speed.

The scores achieved by the internal and external focus groups during practice, retention, and transfer are shown in figure 2.7. While

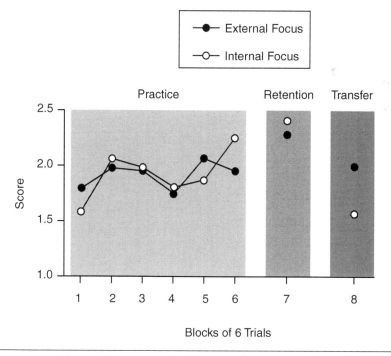

FIGURE 2.7 Accuracy scores of the internal and external focus groups on the soccer task used by Wulf, Wächter, and Wortmann (2003).

Adapted from Women in Sport and Physical Activity Journal Vol. 12, No 1 (2003) with permission from the National Association for Girls and Women in Sport (NAGWS), 1900 Association Drive, Reston, VA 20191-1599.

there were no significant differences between the groups during practice or retention, the transfer results were interesting. In general, scores were lower on the transfer test, which is not too surprising given that the task was more difficult. Yet the internal focus group demonstrated a greater performance decrement from the retention to the transfer test than did the external focus group. In fact, the external focus group performed significantly better than the internal focus group on the novel transfer task. Thus, the instructions we gave during practice influenced performance on a novel, and more difficult, task. This is particularly interesting given that the study was conducted in a classroom setting, where a host of other factors can potentially affect performance, including observing and being observed by others, competition, social comparison, and motivational effects that may positively or negatively affect learning in group situations. The results show that despite the potential influence of these factors, the learners' focus of attention still affected learning.

TENNIS

The golf, basketball free-throw, and soccer studies, as well as the ski simulator and stabilometer studies, involved so-called closed skills that are performed in a relatively stable environment. That is, the environmental conditions typically do not change unpredictably during performance. Also, the performer can often initiate his or her movements at will. Closed skills include those required in gymnastics, diving, golf, swimming, track and field, archery, and so forth. Closed skills are viewed as being at one end of a continuum, with so-called open skills at the other end. Open skills are characterized by the fact that they are performed in an unstable environment. Open skills are prevalent, for example, in ball games in which teammates and opponent constantly change positions, and in sports that are performed outdoors, where wind, waves, or other weather conditions may change during the execution of the skill. Most skills lie somewhere between the two extremes of the continuum, such that small changes, or changes that are not completely unpredictable, can occur.

We have already seen that the learning of closed skills can benefit from an external focus of attention. An interesting question was whether external focus advantages would also be seen for open skills, in which the performer has to coordinate her or his actions in accordance with the movements of an object to be acted upon or those of a partner or opponent. Because actions are performed in response to a moving object such as an oncoming ball (or a moving person), there is typically not much time to plan them, and they tend to be relatively fast. This also means that open skills are often performed under time pressure. Would participants still be able to focus on what was instructed under these constraints? And would the external focus advantage also be seen under these conditions?

In 1999, Dianne Maddox, a graduate student of Professor David Wright's at Texas A&M University, did a study using tennis backhand strokes to examine this question (Maddox, Wulf, & Wright, 1999). She asked novice tennis players in one of the tennis classes she taught to hit tennis balls into a target area. In fact, she had participants get together in pairs, with one person tossing the balls to his or her partner from the other side of the court. Thus, there was necessarily some variability in the timing and in the direction, length, and height of the ball trajectories. External focus participants were instructed to focus on the (anticipated) trajectory of the ball they would hit and its landing point, while internal focus participants were instructed to focus on their backswing and where they hit the ball relative to their front foot (internal focus). The results showed that the external focus participants were clearly more accurate in their shots than the internal focus group. Also, these learning advantages in the movement outcome were not achieved at the expense of the movement form, as the two groups turned out to be similar in the quality of their movement technique. Thus, an external focus can also be beneficial for open skills—despite the large amount of information individuals need to process (e.g., the speed, direction, and perhaps spin of the ball, their position in relation to the ball) *and* despite the relatively short time periods available in those sports for focusing their attention.

JUMPING

Most previous studies of attentional focus effects have used relatively complex motor skills that required the coordination of multiple degrees of freedom, that were fairly challenging, and that often showed considerable improvement across trials. In another study that Zachry did in our lab (Wulf, Zachry, Granados, & Dufek, 2006, Experiment 1), she wanted to examine whether the external focus benefits would generalize to a task that most adult participants already had in their repertoire of motor skills and that seemed to depend mainly on maximum force production, namely, a vertical jump-and-reach task. Would instructing individuals to adopt an external focus increase jump height compared to internal focus or no attentional focus instructions?

Zachry had participants perform a jump-and-reach task using a Vertec measurement device (see photo). Participants were instructed to jump straight up and touch the highest rung on the Vertec they could reach with the tips of the fingers. Each participant performed five trials under one of three conditions: control, internal focus, and external focus. For the control condition, no attentional focus instructions were given. Under the internal focus condition, participants were instructed to concentrate on the tips of their fingers. Under the external focus condition they were instructed to concentrate on the object to be touched, that is, the rungs of the Vertec.

Participant performing a jump-and-reach task with the Vertec measurement device.

Participants indeed reached higher rungs when they adopted an external focus (on average, 4.79 rungs) compared to an internal focus (4.12 rungs) or when they had received no attentional focus instructions (4.10 rungs). Also, the time they spent in the air was longer under the external (0.491 s) than under the internal focus (0.477 s) or the control condition (0.478 s). Thus, a change in the focus of attention significantly affected maximum reach height: Focusing on the object to be touched resulted in more effective performance than did focusing on the finger with which the object was to be touched. Perhaps most interestingly, instructing participants to adopt an external focus increased jump height above and beyond what participants achieved under "normal" conditions (i.e., control conditions without instructions). These results were recently replicated by Carolina Granados in my lab (Wulf, Zachry, Granados, & Dufek, 2006, Experiment 2). In addition to looking at reach height, Granados calculated the displacement of participants' center of mass during the jumps. Interestingly, she found not only the greatest reach heights under the external focus condition, but also greater vertical displacements of the center of mass (0.51 m) compared to those in the internal focus (0.47 m) and control conditions (0.47 m).

These findings might seem surprising given that one might expect the jump height to be determined mainly (although not exclusively) by the participant's strength. Yet we also know, for example, that the coordination between and within muscles influences maximum force production as well (Hollmann & Hettinger, 2000). It is possible that an external focus optimizes those coordination patterns. While we have to await further research to find out how exactly the attentional focus instructions affected jump height, the findings of this study could have implications for sports in which maximum forces must be generated in a short period of time (e.g., high jump, long jump, pole vault, basketball layup). In those cases, focusing on the target (e.g., the bar in high jump) might also result in more effective performance than focusing on movement coordination or not focusing on anything in particular.

ATTENTIONAL INSIGHTS

While it is exciting to see experimental evidence for the benefits of an external focus for a wide range of skills, hearing from friends and colleagues that an external focus "works" for them is at least as satisfying. For example, Bill Prinzmetal, a professor of psychology at the University of California at Berkeley and a fellow windsurfer, recently

(continued)

shared his experience in a letter to the editor of the magazine *Windsurfing*. The following is an excerpt from his letter:

> The traditional approach is to worry about your body mechanics, what she calls 'internal focus'. People talk about 'muscle memory', and making your body 'do' the right thing. Professor Wulf has shown in numerous studies that there is a much better way. Think about the goal of your actions, what she calls 'external focus'. The idea is that your brain knows how to efficiently and largely unconsciously achieve a goal, but is very bad at consciously following a plan.
>
> Let me give one example, applied to windsurfing. I own every jibe video ever made in English and have taken a number of wonderful seminars and lessons. In almost every case, the instructions for entering the jibe have something like assume a 'bow and arrow' or 'playing pool' position. The front arm should be straight, the sail sheeted in with the back arm. Weight should be forward on the board.
>
> Go to a windy spot and see how many people actually have their front arm straight. Practically none. I would go into a turn, and 'command' my arm to straighten out, but it refused! That is an internal focus, and it doesn't work very well.
>
> The alternative is 'external focus,' give your body a goal, and it will achieve the goal. I tell myself that I want to put the rig in a particular position: I want it so that if I were to drop a line straight down from the boom clamp, it would be about 8" in front of the universal, and slightly to leeward of the center of the board. . . . This position is easy to accomplish, because it is a clear goal for your body to achieve: It's as simple as picking up a saltshaker and placing it at a particular position on a table. I just have to place the boom clamp in a particular position over a spot on the board. I am not focused on my body, but the boom position.
>
> When I wasn't thinking about my body, but the goal (boom clamp in a certain position), the results were amazing. My front arm was straight, for perhaps the first

time. This resulted in my sheeting in (without thinking about it), and my weight forward. I flew around the turn so fast that I was shocked.

There are other examples that apply to windsurfing. For example, I do not think about weighting the inside edge of the board, but rather the board inclination. My body 'knows' how to achieve this goal, when it's freed of micromanagement!

OTHER SKILLS

We have already seen a number of examples of how an external focus can enhance the performance and learning of motor skills. However, most of the studies comparing the effectiveness of different types of foci have used skills that require an implement or involve the use of an object in the environment (e.g., racket, club, ball, moving support surface); in these cases the performer can easily focus on the (intended) movement effect on the implement or object. Therefore, people have often asked me what one should focus on if the skill doesn't have an obvious effect on the environment, such as many skills in gymnastics, dance, or diving. This, of course, is a legitimate question. One possibility in these cases would be to use analogies or metaphors. Similar to what happens with an external focus, these tend to distract the performer's attention from her or his body movements, at the same time providing a mental image of the movement goal. For example, if swimmers have used fins before (i.e., in swimming the crawl, backstroke, or butterfly), they could be instructed to imagine their feet as fins. This might automatically trigger the correct foot and leg action without inducing too much conscious control. Providing the performer with a "picture" of (part of) the skill might require some creativity but is likely to produce results similar to those with external focus instructions.

Tables 2.3 through 2.6 present examples of different types of skills from different performance contexts, including sports, therapy (physical, occupational, speech), and music, and possible internal and external foci for each skill. The tables, which are based on Gentile's (1987) taxonomy of motor skills, include skills that require, or do not require, the manipulation of an object. In addition, the tables include skills that involve a change in body location (body transport) or

TABLE 2.3　BODY STABILITY WITH NO OBJECT MANIPULATION

Performance context	Sports					
Goal	Handstand		Performing arm motion of breaststroke while standing		Performing tennis shots without a racket	
Instructions	**Internal focus**	**External focus**	**Internal focus**	**External focus**	**Internal focus**	**External focus**
	Straight body	Inverted pendulum	Hand movements	Producing a triangle	Arm movement	Movement of imagined racket
Performance context	**Physical therapy, occupational therapy, speech therapy**					
Goal	Standing		Speaking (persons with apraxia of speech)		Sit-to-stand	
Instructions	**Internal focus**	**External focus**	**Internal focus**	**External focus**	**Internal focus**	**External focus**
	Pressure on each foot	Pressure exerted on support surface	Posture of tongue	Air released from plosives	Lean forward, extend hips and legs	Stand up to reach for an imaginary object
Performance context	**Music, performing arts**					
Goal	Whistling		Singing		Public speaking	
Instructions	**Internal focus**	**External focus**	**Internal focus**	**External focus**	**Internal focus**	**External focus**
	Lip aperture	Produced sound	Tension of the vocal cords	Notes' reverberative qualities	Vibratory sensations from vocal cords	Projection of voice

Based on Gentile 1987.

TABLE 2.4 BODY STABILITY WITH OBJECT MANIPULATION

Performance context	Sports					
Goal	Throwing a javelin		Shooting free throws in basketball		Riding a motorcycle on winding road	
Instructions	Internal focus	External focus	Internal focus	External focus	Internal focus	External focus
	Arm movement	Movement of the javelin	Wrist flexion	Ball rotation	Leaning body into curves	Lean of motorcycle
Performance context	Physical therapy, occupational therapy					
Goal	Handwriting with Parkinson's disease		Tying a knot after stroke		Moving an object on a table after stroke	
Instructions	Internal focus	External focus	Internal focus	External focus	Internal focus	External focus
	Steady hand movements	Words written on paper	Hands	Cords	Hand and finger movements	Position of the object
Performance context	Music, performing arts					
Goal	Playing the flute		Playing the drums		Juggling	
Instructions	Internal focus	External focus	Internal focus	External focus	Internal focus	External focus
	Accurate finger movements	Quality of sound	Wrist movements	Movements of sticks	Movement of hands	Movement of objects

Based on Gentile 1987.

TABLE 2.5   BODY TRANSPORT WITH NO OBJECT MANIPULATION

Performance context	Sports					
Goal	Jumping forward on one leg		Somersault		Performing a dance routine	
Instructions	Internal focus	External focus	Internal focus	External focus	Internal focus	External focus
	Maintaining balance on foot	(Imagined) targets on floor	Moving limbs close to center of mass	Fast rotation	Individual steps	Movement path
Performance context	**Physical therapy, occupational therapy**					
Goal	Walking after stroke		Running after knee surgery		Hopping after ankle injury	
Instructions	Internal focus	External focus	Internal focus	External focus	Internal focus	External focus
	Equal weight distribution	Producing big steps	Knee extension in injured leg	Distance covered with each step	Ankle extension	Height of jumps
Performance context	**Performing arts**					
Goal	Performing a spin in ice dancing		Performing a jump sequence		Walking on a theater stage	
Instructions	Internal focus	External focus	Internal focus	External focus	Internal focus	External focus
	Arm position	Speed of rotation	Jumping high	Height of the jumps	Body posture	Mood one is trying to portray

Based on Gentile 1987.

TABLE 2.6   BODY TRANSPORT WITH OBJECT MANIPULATION

Performance context	Sports					
Goal	Dribbling a soccer ball through pylons		Downhill skiing		Jibe in windsurfing	
Instructions	**Internal focus**	**External focus**	**Internal focus**	**External focus**	**Internal focus**	**External focus**
	Part of foot contacting the ball	Part of ball being contacted	Weight distribution on feet	Pressure on tips of skis	Pressure exerted on board	Tilt of board
Performance context	**Physical therapy, occupational therapy**					
Goal	Carrying a cup of coffee		Swimming		Walking with a walker	
Instructions	**Internal focus**	**External focus**	**Internal focus**	**External focus**	**Internal focus**	**External focus**
	Keeping hand still	Keeping cup still	Arm motion	Pushing water back	Step length	Placement of walker
Performance context	**Music, performing arts**					
Goal	Playing the trumpet in a marching band		Baton twirling in a marching band		Walking a tightrope	
Instructions	**Internal focus**	**External focus**	**Internal focus**	**External focus**	**Internal focus**	**External focus**
	Lip pressure	Clear tone	Force produced with arm	Height of the baton	Hands	Balance pole

Based on Gentile 1987.

that do not involve a change in location (body stability). (Gentile's taxonomy also differentiates between skills that require movement variations from trial to trial or do not, as well as skills that take place in stable ["closed skills"] or variable environments ["open skills"], but these are not considered in the tables as they would not affect the focus instructions.)

DISTANCE EFFECTS

As we have seen, the benefits of focusing on the movement effect, as compared to the actual coordination of one's movements, appear to be quite robust. They have been shown for a variety of skills as well as in different settings. Also, the movement effects or the body movements that participants were instructed to focus on were obviously different for different tasks. In our studies, we typically chose to direct individuals' attention to those aspects of the skill that were generally considered critical components of the skill. Many skills have more than one effect that a person could focus on, however. For example, a golfer might focus on the club motion, the anticipated ball trajectory, or the intended final position of the ball. A pianist might focus on the key she has to strike or on the sounds she wants to produce.

One might therefore ask whether different external foci might also differ in their effectiveness. If you look back at some of the studies discussed earlier, you'll see that the magnitude of the external focus advantage seemed to vary across different tasks. More specifically, the beneficial effect of an external focus of attention seemed to vary as a function of the *distance* of the effect from the body movements that produced it. For example, on the stabilometer task (e.g., Wulf, Höß, & Prinz, 1998, Experiment 2), where the distance between the feet and the markers on the platform was extremely small (in fact, the feet touched the markers), the advantage of the external focus (markers) compared to the internal focus (feet) became apparent only on the retention test after two days of practice. The fact that the distance between the cues that participants focused on in the two conditions was so minimal might be one reason why performance differences between groups became apparent relatively late. On the ski simulator task (Wulf, Höß, & Prinz, 1998, Experiment 1), the internal and external cues were presumably somewhat more distinct, as the wheels (external focus) were located under the feet (internal focus). In this case, the external focus benefits were first seen at the end of the first day of practice. Finally, in the golf studies (Wulf, Lauterbach, & Toole, 1999; Wulf & Su, in press), the advantage of the external focus showed up almost immediately, that is, within the first 10 practice trials or so. Here, the distance between the arms (internal focus) and the club, in particular the club head (external focus), was even greater. Thus, is it possible that increasing the distance of the movement effect from the body might accentuate the advantages of an external relative to an internal focus of attention? If so, why would something as apparently trivial as the spatial distance between an action and its effect have such a profound influence on how well we learn a task? We suspected that effects occurring in close spatial proximity to the body are less easily distinguishable from the body than are more remote effects. On the basis of this observation, we speculated that a greater distance between the body and the effect produced by its movements might further enhance the learning advantage associated with an external focus of attention (McNevin, Shea, & Wulf, 2003).

To test this hypothesis, we used the stabilometer task and manipulated the distance of the external movement effects, that is, the markers that we asked participants to direct their attention to. Two markers were placed on the platform in about the same position as in the earlier studies (e.g., Wulf, Höß, & Prinz, 1998, Experiment 2). All participants, independent of their group assignment, were instructed to place their feet behind these markers. We called these the "near" markers, as they were near the feet (see figure 2.8). In addition to these markers, we attached two other pairs of markers to the platform. One set of markers was placed 26 cm (10 in.) to the outside of the markers in front of the feet, whereas the other set was placed inside of these markers and next to the midline of the platform. We referred to these as the far-outside and far-inside markers, respectively.

Note that participants did not visually monitor the position of the markers. Rather, they were instructed to look at the wall in front of them, and to just focus their attention on—or imagine—the position of the respective markers. If the distance of the effect from the body is indeed a variable that has a modifying influence on the strength of the attentional focus effect, participants who focused on either the far-outside or far-inside markers should show comparable performances, as the two marker sets were located at about the same distance from the feet. Also, we expected both "far" groups to outperform the "near" group. Finally, we added an internal focus

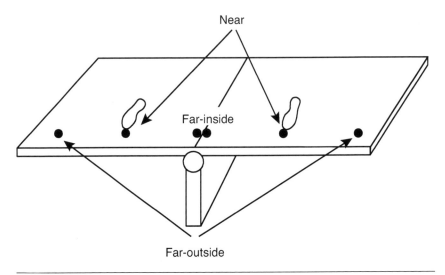

FIGURE 2.8 Marker placement in the study by McNevin, Shea, and Wulf (2003).

Reprinted, by permission, from N.H. McNevin, C.H. Shea, and G. Wulf, 2003, "Increasing the distance of an external focus of attention enhances learning," *Psychological Research* 67: 22-29.

control group that was instructed to focus on their feet, as in earlier studies. The performance of those participants was expected to be less effective than that of all external focus groups.

Figure 2.9 shows the deviations from the horizontal (root-mean-square error) for the four groups during two days of practice and the retention test on Day 3. As you can see, all groups improved considerably during practice. The most interesting results are those of the retention test, though (for which no attentional focus instructions were given). An internal focus resulted in significantly larger deviations than all external focus conditions (far outside, far inside, near), replicating our earlier findings that an external focus is generally more effective than an internal focus. More interestingly, though, the two groups that focused on the distant markers (far outside, far inside) were clearly more effective at maintaining their balance than the groups that focused on the markers close to the feet (near). Furthermore, the far-outside and far-inside groups showed very similar performances, indicating that the distance from the body is the critical factor, and not, for example, the direction of the effect in relation to the body or the (imagined) amount of displacement of the markers. (For any given rotation of the platform, the far-outside markers displace more than markers placed in front of the feet, and

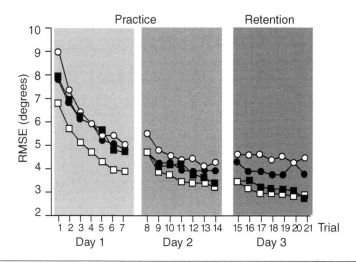

FIGURE 2.9 Deviations of the stabilometer platform from the horizontal (root-mean-square error) for the internal, far-inside, near, and far-outside groups in the study by McNevin, Shea, and Wulf (2003).

Reprinted, by permission, from N.H. McNevin, C.H. Shea, and G. Wulf, 2003, "Increasing the distance of an external focus of attention enhances learning," *Psychological Research* 67: 22-29.

more than near markers, which are closer to the axis of rotation). Thus, focusing on the more remote effects indeed turned out to be more beneficial than focusing on effects closer to the body—presumably because more remote effects are easier to discriminate from the body movements that produced them.

In a follow-up study, Jin-Hoon Park, a doctoral student in Charlie Shea's lab, placed a pair of markers at an even greater distance from the feet than in our previous study (Park et al., 2000). He attached markers to the ends of two rods that were about 1 m (1 yd) long and that extended from the stabilometer platform in front of the participant's feet. Interestingly, balance performance was enhanced even further when participants were instructed to focus on those markers!

While it remains to be seen whether or to what extent these findings generalize to other skills, the results suggest that if an action has more than one effect, and these effects differ in their distance from the body, it might be more beneficial for the performer to focus on a more distant effect. For example, motorcyclists are often told to focus on the endpoint of a turn they are negotiating instead of focusing on leaning their body, or the bike, into the turn. Bikers know from experience that this is a more effective strategy—especially in somewhat dangerous and therefore stressful situations (e.g., narrow or wet roads, obstacles in the field of vision)—than directing one's attention internally (body) or to a close effect (motorcycle). If you are a skier, try to focus on the turn *following* the one you are about to make, and you will probably find that it works better than focusing on the immediate turn. Also, focusing on the pressure you are exerting on the tips of your skis is more effective than focusing on the part of the ski under your foot, or on the pressure you are exerting with the respective leg. In tennis, it might be more advantageous to focus on the desired trajectory of the ball as compared to the racket or arm motion.

Whether an external focus on a relatively close (e.g., tennis racket) or more distant effect (e.g., anticipated ball trajectory) is more beneficial might also depend on the performer's level of expertise. In general, it seems to make sense to assume that experts would benefit more from focusing on more remote as compared to close effects; this might "trigger" the whole action necessary to achieve the desired effect. A focus on a distant movement effect might also be advantageous for beginners—provided that the effect is directly related to the body movements that produced it or to effects in close proximity to the body, such as the markers attached to the stabilometer or the angle at which the motorcycle is leaning. However, in cases in which the same effect (e.g., the trajectory of the tennis ball) could, in principle, be achieved with different movement patterns, it would seem that a novice should focus on a closer movement effect (e.g., the movement of the racket) in order to develop an effective and reliable movement pattern first. In chapter 5, we will discuss in more detail how attentional focus effects may vary as a function of expertise.

INDIVIDUAL DIFFERENCES

When I first presented our findings on the effects of internal versus external foci of attention at conferences, some scientists were skeptical as to the generalizability of the external focus benefits across individuals. Some people raised the question whether there might be individual differences in the preference for, and perhaps in the effectiveness of, the type of attentional focus. It is well known that athletes develop their own attentional strategies. One basketball player might, for example, focus on the backboard when shooting free throws, while another might focus on the wrist motion. Is it possible that for one performer an external focus might be more effective, whereas for another performer an internal focus works better? Even if an external focus is more effective for most people, some individuals might have a preference for an internal focus and might benefit more from adopting an internal focus. Alternatively, the advantage of concentrating on the effects of one's movements, rather than on the movements themselves, might be a relatively general phenomenon. It seemed important to examine this issue. If, indeed, some individuals have a preference for an internal focus and show similar benefits if allowed to adopt an internal focus, no difference between participants with external versus internal focus preferences should be found. If, however, the benefits of an external focus are robust and independent of individual differences, participants with an external focus should show superior learning relative to those with an internal focus. We therefore conducted a study to examine these questions (Wulf, Shea, & Park, 2001). Another purpose of that study was to determine whether learners are sensitive to the effectiveness of different attentional foci if given a chance to compare them directly.

In our study, we gave participants the option to adopt an internal or external focus of attention (Wulf, Shea, & Park, 2001). That is, we asked participants to find out for themselves which type of attentional focus would work better for them. In the first experiment, participants practicing to balance on the stabilometer were asked to switch their focus of attention between internal (feet) and external (markers on the platform) from trial to trial on Day 1. At the end of the first practice phase, we asked them to choose the attentional focus that was best for them. On the second day of practice, we instructed them to utilize only their preferred attentional focus. On Day 3, we conducted a retention test to see if there were any learning differences between people who preferred an internal versus external focus. Also, at the end of the retention test, we interviewed participants to determine whether they had indeed used their preferred attentional focus during retention, or whether they had focused on something else, and if so, what.

The interview results revealed that, despite the initial preference for an internal relative to an external focus at the end of Day 1 (of the 17 participants, 10 chose to focus on their feet, whereas 7 participants decided to focus on the markers), a considerably greater number of participants ended up choosing an external (12 participants) over an internal focus (5 participants) in retention. Most importantly, individuals who adopted an external focus on the retention test also showed better balance performance than those who chose an internal focus.

These results suggested that the differential effects of an external versus internal attentional focus might become visible and noticeable for learners only after a certain amount of practice (at least on this task, where the distance between feet and markers was minimal; see section "Distance Effects"). Thus, it might not be too surprising that there was no clear preference for an external focus after one day of practice, with only half of the trials being devoted to either focus. Therefore, we conducted a second experiment. We asked a group of 20 individuals to find out whether focusing on their feet (internal focus) or on two markers in front of their feet (external focus) was more effective. However, this time we gave participants two days of practice. In addition, there were no restrictions as to when they were to focus internally or externally during the practice phase. Rather, during each practice trial they were asked to indicate whether they were concentrating on the feet or on the markers and when they switched from one to the other. The experimenter recorded these times. Only at the end of the second day, participants were asked whether they preferred an internal or external focus. On the retention test (Day 3), we instructed them to use only the focus of attention they had found to be more effective on the first two days.

We were again interested in how many participants would prefer each type of focus. In addition, we wanted to know how much time they spent focusing externally or internally during practice, as a preference for a certain focus might manifest itself also in longer time periods spent with that strategy during practice. Finally, of course, we were interested in the retention performances of those who had chosen an external versus internal focus.

It turned out that a considerably greater number of participants, namely 16 out of 20, chose an external focus rather than an internal focus. This shows that most people were indeed sensitive to the differential effects of the type of focus after two days of trying out both. Interestingly, even though participants were repeatedly encouraged to try out both attentional strategies, those who eventually decided to focus their attention on the markers spent more time during practice concentrating on the markers than on their feet, and those who eventually chose to focus on the feet spent more time during practice concentrating on their feet. Finally, and most importantly, those participants who chose to focus on the markers were clearly superior at balancing than those who focused on their feet.

Learners' preferences for external focus instructions are also reflected in the results of a questionnaire used by Marchant, Clough, and Crawshaw (in press). As described earlier, in that study novices performed a dart throwing task. The study also involved a questionnaire in which participants were asked several questions, including "How successful do you think these instructions were in making your dart throws accurate?" On a scale from 1 (low) to 5 (high), participants who were given external focus instructions rated the success of their instructions 3.4, whereas participants with internal focus instructions rated their instructions 2.7. The difference in performers' ratings was statistically significant. (Control group participants, who were not given focus instructions, rated their instructions as 3.0, which was not significantly different from the rating of either attentional focus group.) As already mentioned, external focus participants were indeed more accurate in their throws than internal focus participants. Thus, as in the study by Wulf, Shea, and Park (2001), participants were sensitive to the effectiveness of the instructions. It is interesting to note that, unlike participants in the Wulf, Shea, and Park study, learners in the study by Marchant and colleagues were assigned to different groups (internal vs. external focus) and thus did not have the opportunity to directly compare the effects of the different instructions. Yet, the results were similar: As in the experiments of Wulf and colleagues, in which most participants indicated that the external focus worked better for them, those in the study by Marchant and colleagues who had experienced an external focus rated its success higher than those who had experienced an internal focus.

Overall, it seems that one can discount the notion that individual differences play a significant role in the relative effectiveness of an external versus internal focus of attention. Rather, most performers noticed the differential effectiveness of internal versus external foci, independent of initial preferences they might have had. Thus, the benefits of an external focus appear to be a relatively general phenomenon and not one that is qualified by individual differences.

If you have ever tried to ride a unicycle, you know that trying to "remain in balance" does not work. However, focusing on where you want to go does!

PERFORMANCE VERSUS LEARNING

The studies we have discussed so far provide converging evidence that adopting an external focus is more effective than adopting an internal focus. An important issue, however, is whether the external focus advantage is "just" a temporary performance effect or whether it is a more permanent, or learning, effect. That is, does it occur only when individuals are actually focusing externally, or would it also be seen later when people do not maintain the external focus anymore? Even if this benefit occurred only while people were performing with an external focus, this would be an important result and would have considerable practical implications. Yet it would be even more impressive and important if one could show that practicing a task with an external focus resulted in benefits even if people didn't use that focus anymore. Remember, learning is typically assessed in retention tests, in which no attentional focus instructions or reminders are given. However, in studies on attentional focus, one often cannot be sure that participants don't use the same focus in retention tests that they were instructed to use during practice. One way to avoid this problem is to *prevent* people from using that focus. Indeed, there have been a couple of studies in which learners could not use the focus they had adopted during practice, and those studies show that the external focus effects are, in fact, relatively permanent effects.

In one study, a former student of mine at the University of Reading (United Kingdom), Vaso Totosika, used a Pedalo (see photo on page 76). The task involves coordination of the whole body and is primarily a balance task. The Pedalo is often used for balance training in therapeutic settings, especially with children. It is also a great apparatus to use to demonstrate external versus internal focus differences in motor behavior classes at the university level. Asking students to try it out with a focus on pushing their feet forward (internal), or on pushing the platforms forward (external), almost always results in the same answer when students are asked which focus "works" better. Almost without exception, students will respond that focusing on the platforms makes the task easier. That is, the difference in the effectiveness of the two attentional focus strategies is obvious almost immediately.

In her study, Totosika had two groups of participants practice the Pedalo task with either an external (platforms) or internal focus of attention (feet) (Totosika & Wulf, 2003). Specifically, she asked participants to ride a distance of 15 m (16.4 yd) at their "own pace." Nevertheless, she measured the time they needed from the start to the finish line. All participants had 20 practice trials. Not surprisingly, participants generally became faster with practice. But more importantly, people who were instructed to adopt an external focus were faster than people who adopted an internal focus. As mentioned before, an important aspect of this study was to examine whether this advantage of an external focus would also be seen if people were prevented from focusing in the same way they had during practice (on platforms or feet). Therefore, Totosika gave them a secondary task to perform while riding the Pedalo: They had to count backward by threes loudly from a two-digit number that was given to them by the experimenter. In addition, this time they had to ride the Pedalo as fast as possible. Thus, the question was, would people who had practiced with an external focus still be faster when they were "distracted" by the counting-backward task and therefore unable to maintain their focus? The results were clear. Having practiced with an external focus resulted in faster movement times than having practiced with an internal focus—even when attention had to be directed to something else.

These findings are important, because they show that the differential effects of external versus internal foci of attention are not just temporary influences on performance but are indeed learning effects. (Another study that nicely demonstrates the relatively permanent benefits of an external focus will be discussed in chapter 6.) These results are noteworthy in relation to many real-life

The Pedalo consists of three pairs of wheels and two platforms between them. It moves when the rider alternately pushes the upper platform forward and downward, similarly to the pedals on a bicycle.

situations. Often we have to perform under stressful conditions, or in situations in which we are distracted by spectators, competitors, or just our own thoughts. It is comforting to know that the benefits resulting from having practiced with an external focus will still be there.

As an aside, in the same study Totosika found that the effects of having practiced with an external focus also generalized to two other novel conditions: riding the Pedalo under time pressure ("Ride as fast as you can") and riding it backward under time pressure ("Ride backwards as fast as you can"). In both of those transfer tests, external focus participants were faster than internal focus participants. Together with the transfer test results of the soccer study discussed earlier (Wulf, Wächter, & Wortmann, 2003; see section "Soccer"), these findings demonstrate that the benefits of practice with an external focus are not restricted to the practiced task but generalize to other variations of that skill.

SUMMARY

The studies we have reviewed in this chapter confirm the anecdotal observation (in windsurfing) that the performance of motor skills seems to be more effective if one focuses on the effects one's movements have on the environment rather than on the movements themselves. The results from studies using various laboratory tasks as well as sport skills provide converging evidence for the advantages of instructions that induce an external relative to an internal focus. The benefits of an external focus appear to be even more pronounced if the movement effect occurs at a distance from the body, thus making it more easily distinguishable from the body movements that produced it. Furthermore, this effect seems to be rather general and not dependent on individual preferences. In fact, performers often notice immediate changes in their performance as a function of their focus of attention. Importantly, the effects of adopting an external focus when practicing a skill is not just temporary, that is, present only when the individual adopts that focus; rather, these benefits are seen in the retention of the skill and in transfer to novel variations of the skill. In the next chapter, we will examine whether the effectiveness of feedback might also depend on the type of attentional focus it induces.

Practical Applications

Sport Implements

Many sport skills involve objects, such as balls, and implements to strike these objects with (e.g., tennis or badminton rackets, baseball bats, golf clubs, hockey sticks). There are also javelins, discuses, hammers, skis, surfboards, skateboards, unicycles, and apparatuses in gymnastics, as well as targets (baskets, goals, bull's eyes, holes). According to the findings discussed in this chapter, the learning of such skills should benefit if the performer's attention is directed to effects of his or her movements on the object, rather than to the body movements producing those effects.

- Pick a favorite sport and list the considerations for the objects involved. Then, discuss the tactics that a coach needs to provide to an athlete, with appropriate instructions that take into consideration attentional focus research.

Metaphors

Some sport activities don't involve objects, for example a floor routine in gymnastics, or springboard diving, or swimming. In those cases, the use of metaphors or analogies might be beneficial. As with instructions that direct attention to the movement effect on the environment, they can provide an image of the movement outcome that the individual can attempt to produce without focusing on the movements themselves. Masters (2000) has suggested the use of an analogy for teaching a top-spun forehand in table tennis. Learners are asked to imagine a right-handed triangle and to bring the racket squarely up the hypotenuse. This allows the performer to focus on the desired effect without worrying about the details of the coordination pattern.

- What instruction could a gymnastics coach give an athlete performing a handstand in order to facilitate the maintenance of balance, or a gymnast doing a twist to remain in a vertical position?
- Can you think of a metaphor a swim instructor could give a novice swimmer who is learning the arm motion for the back crawl?

Distance

In some situations, it might be possible to take advantage of the "distance" effect. If attention can be directed to a movement effect that occurs at a greater distance from the body, compared to one that is close to the body, the benefits might be even more pronounced. For example, in downhill skiing, a skier could be instructed to exert pressure on the *tips* of the skis (to gain better control over the speed and make the skis run more smoothly on "bumpy" snow), rather than being told to lean forward. Furthermore, in slalom skiing, simply focusing on "turning" might elicit the appropriate action in a skilled skier, whereas a somewhat less skilled person might want to focus on the skis turning—perhaps even imagining that the skis are on rails to facilitate a parallel turn. (All of these strategies have been shown to "work" in personal testing!)

- Which other skills have effects at different distances from the body, and how could you give instructions that take advantage of the "distance effect"?
- Would you vary the instructions for novices versus more advanced performers?

FINE MOTOR SKILLS

The advantages of an external focus should not be limited to sport skills, but should extend to other motor skills as well, for example, those required in surgery or musical performance. For example, endoscopy is a medical procedure that requires fine motor skills. By inserting a scope into the body, the surgeon is able to see the interior surface of an organ. In addition, instruments can be inserted to take biopsies or retrieve foreign objects. Given the beneficial effects of an external focus shown in the studies reviewed in this chapter, Thuraisingam, Levine, and Andersen (2006) suggested that the training of surgeons could perhaps be improved by instructions that direct attention to the endoscopic view (e.g., "look up") rather than to the movements of the hands (e.g., "thumb down on big wheel"). The authors also note that such instructions have anecdotally been shown to be successful in training courses.

People who play musical instruments might benefit from adopting an external focus. The learning process often involves developing a feel for the right amount of pressure by the fingers on the instrument. Instead of directing learners' attention to their fingers, the instructor could direct their attention to the resistance of the instrument, or to the resulting sound (Saxer, 2004). For the flute, for instance, Saxer (2004) suggests having the student practice the finger movements on a piece of cardboard and directing attention to the loudness of the sounds produced. In another example related to the flute, Saxer recommends that instead of instructing people to focus on the tension of the lips, one instruct them to direct attention to the flow of air (produced by the lip opening). Furthermore, the produced sounds are a movement effect that attention can be easily directed to. In fact, the Suzuki Method of music education, which was developed by the Japanese violinist Shinichi Suzuki, makes use of this idea. Suzuki believed that the best way for children to learn to play music was to expose them to it and to have them play it "by ear," without teaching them first how to read music. This way, the child develops an auditory template that he or she can use to produce the desired "effect." This method has been used quite successfully.

- What instructions could a music teacher give a pianist, or a singer, to enhance performance?
- Do you believe an external focus could be helpful in reducing choking in performance situations? If so, why?

FUTURE DIRECTIONS

DISTANCE EFFECTS

While the "distance" effect is intriguing, its generalizability to other skills, including real-life skills, needs to be examined. It would also be interesting to see if an optimal distance of the external focus exists and whether it is different for different skill levels. For example, would experts benefit more from focusing on a more distant effect than from focusing on a closer effect? The difficulty with such studies is that, especially in real-life skills, the distance of the movement effect is often confounded with the type of effect (e.g., most "distant" effects also tend to be "high-level" effects; see also chapter 5). This issue should also be considered in future studies.

TASKS WITH NO OBVIOUS EFFECTS

As of yet, there don't appear to be any studies that have addressed attentional focus effects for skills that don't involve obvious effects on the environment. While this would be more challenging than using skills that have such effects, researchers should make an attempt to examine the effectiveness of different focus instructions on those skills as well.

MOVEMENT FORM

Most attentional focus studies have used outcome measures of performance, such as movement accuracy, amplitude, speed, and various measures of balance or postural sway. Only very few studies have looked at how movement form is affected by the type of attentional focus. An important question is, Does an external focus also enhance movement form? Do learners develop a more effective and efficient technique as a by-product of focusing on the outcome of their movements? Also, how about the stability of the movement pattern as a function of attentional focus? Expert ratings or motion analyses procedures could perhaps be used in future studies to provide a more complete picture of how the focus of attention affects performance.

LONG-TERM EFFECTS

Most studies in the area of motor learning use relatively short retention intervals to determine learning effects. Similarly, the learning studies in the area of attentional focus have used retention intervals that ranged from one to seven days. While this demonstrates that there is some permanency to the effects of attentional focus, future researchers might want to include longer retention intervals to determine long-term effects.

A ski instructor might tell a novice skier to bend her knees more and lean forward, while keeping her weight on the downhill ski.

CHAPTER 3

INTERNAL VERSUS EXTERNAL FOCUS FEEDBACK

Coaches, teachers, and physical therapists often give learners feedback about their performance. Typically, this feedback is directed at certain components of the movement, often those that need the most improvement. That is, on the basis of what the coach considers to be the critical mistake or flaw, he or she gives feedback that is supposed to help the performer make appropriate changes. Consider a novice skier who wants to learn a parallel turn. Her main problem is that she speeds up during the turn and her skis move apart. She has hired a ski instructor to help her improve her technique so that she gets the most out of her four-day skiing vacation. The instructor tells her that she needs to lean forward more and that she should shift her weight more to the outer leg. While this feedback seems to help some, it does not lead to the immediate and substantial improvement the skier had hoped for. She comes to the conclusion that skiing is just a very difficult sport that requires a lot of practice.

Walter Schneider, a psychology professor at the University of Pittsburgh who has published extensively on attention and performance, may have received similar feedback from a ski instructor. In a book chapter (Schneider & Fisk, 1983, p. 133), he shared this personal experience: When he found himself thinking about which foot was carrying his weight in a turn, he noticed "substantial performance decrements (i.e., many falls) for the remainder of the slope."

A performer's focus of attention is influenced not only by instructions (or by what she or he decides to concentrate on), but presumably also by the feedback given. For example, a golf coach might tell a novice golfer who is practicing putting that his arms are bent too much and might ask the golfer to keep his elbows straight. Or a physical therapist might tell a patient who has trouble walking up stairs to bend her hips more and lift her feet higher. As with instructions, it is probably fair to say that the feedback given in practical settings often refers to the coordination of the individual's body movements and therefore induces an internal focus. This suggests an important question: Is the type of attentional focus induced by the feedback relevant to its effectiveness? A few studies have addressed this question. Specifically, a couple of studies have been concerned with feedback that is given concurrently with the movement. This type of feedback, typically given by a computer, provides information about the kinematics of the movement in relation to the goal pattern. Other studies have looked at how the attentional focus induced by the wording of feedback, such as that given by a coach, affects the learning of sport skills. Before we take a look at these studies, let us briefly review how feedback is generally assumed to function in the learning process.

Research regarding the role of feedback in the learning of motor skills has a long history. In fact, for almost a century, researchers have been concerned with how feedback functions and how it can be made more effective so that the learning process is facilitated (e.g., Thorndike, 1914, 1932; for reviews, see Salmoni, Schmidt, & Walter, 1984; Schmidt, 1991; Swinnen, 1996; Wulf & Shea, 2004). (In the research literature, two types of feedback are distinguished: knowledge of results [KR] and knowledge of performance [KP]. KR is feedback provided after the completion of a movement about the outcome with regard to the goal, whereas KP refers to kinematic information about the movement pattern.) Feedback serves as a basis for corrections of errors and guides the performer to the correct movement. Thus, it is generally seen as an important learning variable and as essential in achieving more effective performance as practice continues. In fact, early researchers believed that learning was optimized when feedback was provided frequently, immediately, or precisely (e.g., Bilodeau & Bilodeau, 1958; Bilodeau, Bilodeau, & Shumsky, 1959; Thorndike, 1927; see also Adams, 1971; Schmidt, 1975). Recently, these ideas have been questioned, however, and researchers have suggested that a number of factors come into play when feedback is provided during the learning of motor skills.

A critical review and reappraisal of the early feedback literature was published by Salmoni and colleagues (1984). Among other things, these authors noted that many of the early feedback experiments failed to include retention or transfer tests, arguing that these tests are critical for the assessment of what was learned, unaffected by the temporary influences associated with the different manipulations (see also discussion on performance vs. learning in chapter 2). On the basis of their review, Salmoni and colleagues (1984; see also Schmidt, 1991) proposed the "guidance hypothesis." According to this view, feedback *guides* the performer to the correct movement. However, if feedback is provided too frequently, it can also have negative effects. The learner may become too dependent on the feedback and neglect the processing of (intrinsic) feedback associated with the movement, which he or she will have to rely on when the augmented feedback is no longer available. In addition, frequent feedback has been shown to result in less stable performance during practice because it prompts the performer to correct even small errors (termed "maladaptive short-term correction") that may be due simply to an inherent variability in the motor system. The increased variability in performance during practice hinders the development of a stable movement representation.

Guidance Hypothesis

Positive: ➤ Frequent feedback guides the learner to the correct movement.

Negative: ➤ The learner becomes dependent on the feedback.

Negative: ➤ Frequent feedback promotes "maladaptive short-term corrections."

Since the guidance hypothesis was first proposed, numerous experiments using a variety of feedback manipulations have provided support for it (but see Wulf & Shea, 2004, for limitations of the guidance view). These studies typically used feedback manipulations that were designed to reduce the negative guidance effects of feedback and at the same time encourage learners to attend to and utilize their intrinsic feedback. For example, many of these experiments have shown that reducing the frequency of feedback, such that the percentage of trials followed by feedback is reduced (e.g., to 50% of the trials), can enhance learning. Providing less feedback makes learners less likely to become dependent on it and, at the same time, reduces their propensity to constantly change the movement pattern.

One type of feedback that has been shown to be particularly detrimental to learning is feedback that is provided concurrently with the movement. Concurrent feedback typically has very strong performance-enhancing effects during practice; but clear performance decrements, relative to when feedback is provided after the movement, are seen in retention or transfer tests (e.g., Park, Shea, & Wright, 2000; Schmidt & Wulf, 1997; Vander Linden, Cauraugh, & Greene, 1993; Winstein et al., 1996). Feedback presented concurrently with the movement provides very strong guiding effects but blocks the processing of intrinsic feedback and therefore results in the learning decrements seen in retention and transfer tests.

More recent studies have looked at the role of the attentional focus that is induced by the augmented feedback. These studies examined whether feedback that promotes an external versus an internal focus has differential influences on learning. More specifically, these investigations addressed the effects of concurrent feedback (see next section, "Attentional Focus and Concurrent Feedback"), as well as frequent feedback (section "Sport Skill Learning") provided after the movement, as a function of attentional focus. As we will see, the type of attentional focus plays a significant role when it comes to providing feedback as well. This is important for practical applications and also has implications for theoretical views of feedback (see "Theoretical Implications" and "Practical Applications").

ATTENTIONAL FOCUS AND CONCURRENT FEEDBACK

In the first study that addressed the issue of attentional focus and feedback, Charlie Shea and I used the stabilometer task, represented in figure 3.1 (Shea & Wulf, 1999). Usually this task is performed without additional feedback, as performers are informed that the goal of the task is to keep the balance platform horizontal, or at least as close to horizontal as possible, and they can see or feel the actual position of the platform. Thus, any additional feedback about the deviation from the goal might seem redundant.

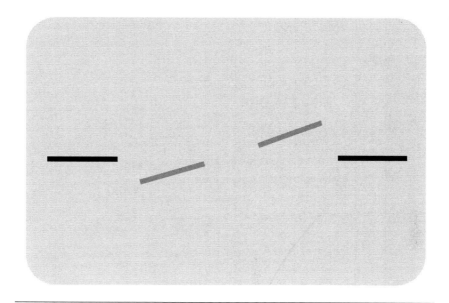

FIGURE 3.1 Feedback provided in the Shea and Wulf (1999) study. The black bars on the outside represent the horizontal reference; the gray bars provide feedback on the position of the platform.

Reprinted from *Human Movement Studies*, Vol. 18, C.H. Shea and G. Wulf, Enhancing motor learning through external-focus instructions and feedback, pgs. 553-571, Copyright 1999, with permission from Elsevier.

Nevertheless, we provided participants with additional (visual) feedback on a computer monitor that was placed in front of the performer (see figure 3.1). The feedback consisted of two black horizontal reference lines on the left and right of the screen and two gray lines (which were actually one line with a gap in the middle) representing deviations of the platform from the horizontal. Figure 3.1 illustrates the feedback display when the left edge of the platform is below horizontal. Thus, in addition to their own intrinsic feedback, participants could see the platform movements on the screen.

To examine whether "external" and "internal" focus feedback would differ in effectiveness, we told one group of participants that the moving lines on the screen should be thought of as representing their feet (feedback/internal focus group), whereas another group was informed that these lines represented the two lines that were marked on the stabilometer platform in front of their feet (feedback/external focus group). In fact, the lines on the platform were present under all conditions, since they also served as markers for the placement of the feet. Participants were instructed to put their feet on the platform so that the tips of their feet touched the lines. Thus, the feedback display was the same for both groups. The only difference between the internal and external feedback groups was their *interpretation* of the feedback. We thought that any benefits of external relative to internal focus feedback would be particularly convincing if they could be demonstrated for *identical* feedback conditions, with participants simply being given different information about the interpretation of the feedback.

As mentioned earlier, though, we were not sure whether the feedback would have any effect at all. If the feedback did not provide augmented information beyond what the performer could derive from her or his intrinsic feedback, it could not be expected to result in additional learning advantages. Some previous studies using ski simulator (Vereijken & Whiting, 1990) or coincidence-timing tasks (Magill, Chamberlin, & Hall, 1991) had shown that feedback is essentially ineffective if it is redundant with the performer's intrinsic feedback. However, we thought that the augmented feedback could also have another function, independent of whether it supposedly referred to the performer's own movements or to the movement effects: It might in and of itself induce an external focus of attention by directing performers' attention to the movement effect (i.e., the feedback). In this case, providing learners with concurrent feedback might—despite its "redundancy"—provide an added benefit, compared to not providing feedback. To find out, we added two conditions without feedback. The two groups that did not receive feedback were instructed to try to keep their feet at the same height (no-feedback/internal focus group) or to try to keep the two lines in front of their feet at the same height (no-feedback/external focus group).

The performances of the four groups are shown in figure 3.2. All groups demonstrated an increased proficiency in performance over the two days of practice; that is, they reduced the average platform deviations from the horizontal (see left and middle panel of figure). What was striking was that the two feedback groups had consistently lower error scores than the no-feedback groups throughout the whole practice phase. The most important results are those of the retention test, though (see right panel of figure). Note that on this retention test, no feedback and no attentional focus instructions were provided. An interesting question was whether the advantages of feedback seen during practice would transfer to

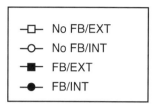

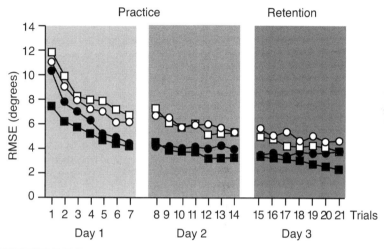

FIGURE 3.2 Deviations of the stabilometer platform from the horizontal (root-mean-square error) for the no-feedback/internal focus, no-feedback/external focus, feedback/internal focus, and feedback/external focus groups (Shea & Wulf, 1999).

a delayed no-feedback retention test. As mentioned earlier, previous studies of concurrent feedback (e.g., Vander Linden, Cauraugh, & Greene, 1993; Schmidt & Wulf, 1997; Winstein et al., 1996) had shown that performance typically deteriorates dramatically when this type of feedback is suddenly removed. This was not the case here, though. The two groups that had received feedback on the first two days again showed more effective balance than the groups without additional feedback. Also, the external focus groups had generally lower error scores than the groups with an internal focus of attention, independent of whether or not they received feedback during practice.

These results demonstrate several important things. First, the external focus feedback was more advantageous than the internal focus feedback. This suggests that the external focus benefits found for instructions earlier indeed generalize to feedback. In this case, this was particularly astounding, though, as the feedback display was identical for the two feedback groups. The implication is that the influence of attentional focus induced by the feedback must be rather strong. Furthermore, the additional feedback provided to learners generally enhanced performers' ability to maintain their balance on the stabilometer—even though the feedback could have been argued to be redundant with their intrinsic feedback. Obviously, learners had visual and kinesthetic feedback available to inform them about the platform's deviation from the horizontal. Yet the visual display of the platform movements on the screen considerably benefited their performance.

How can this be explained? One possible reason for this added benefit of feedback is that it might have represented a more "distal" attentional focus. In chapter 2, we saw that increasing the distance of the external focus can enhance the learning benefit (McNevin, Shea, & Wulf, 2003). The same effect might have played a role here as well. That is, the display information might have served as a more "remote" focal point and generally tended to induce an external focus even when participants were told to think of the feedback as representing their feet. The feedback presumably provided a constant and powerful reminder to maintain an external focus. This might explain why the feedback was generally more effective than the instructions.

Another interesting point regarding the general effectiveness of the concurrent feedback in this study is that besides enhancing performance while it was provided during practice, its beneficial effects were also seen in the retention test without feedback. That is, the feedback not only had a temporary effect on performance but also in fact enhanced the *learning* of this task. On the basis of previous findings, one would not necessarily have expected this (e.g., Vander Linden, Cauraugh, & Greene, 1993; Schmidt & Wulf, 1997; Winstein et al., 1996). When the learner is heavily "guided" by the additional information, he or she typically develops a dependency on it that results in performance decrements when the feedback is no longer available. Such dependency effects seem to occur primarily in "artificial" laboratory tasks, though, in which learners have to rely mainly on the augmented feedback because they are deprived of intrinsic feedback (Wulf & Shea, 2004). In our study, learners apparently did not become dependent on the additional feedback, as performance was maintained in its absence. Both the fact that the feedback in

this experiment considerably enhanced performance during practice (even though it was redundant with the performer's intrinsic
feedback), and the fact that there was no performance decrement
for the feedback groups when feedback was withdrawn in retention, indicate that the function of augmented feedback is not only
informational. Rather, these findings suggest that feedback can also
induce an external focus of attention that benefits performance and
learning. The feedback display may have been sufficient to direct the
learners' attention away from engaging in the active control of their
movements independent of the information, if any, provided by the
feedback. These findings are important, because in many real-world
situations, feedback is often given in addition to the performer's
intrinsic feedback. The results of this study suggest that concurrent
feedback can actually be beneficial in these cases if it induces an
external focus of attention.

Interestingly, a study by Hodges and Franks (2001) showed similar effects. Even though the study did not specifically concern the

© Getty Images

In many real-world situations outside of the laboratory, such as learning to fly,
feedback is given in addition to the performer's intrinsic feedback.

ability of feedback to induce an external versus internal focus, the two types of feedback compared in that experiment can be interpreted as having done so. Similar to the situation in the study by Hodges and Lee (1999) described in chapter 1, participants had to learn a new bimanual coordination pattern by manipulating two levers. Specifically, continuous flexion and extension movements of the two arms were required, with one arm leading the other by a quarter of a cycle (i.e., 90°). If the pattern was produced correctly, it created a circle on a computer screen. (If both arms moved "in" and "out" at the same time, in a so-called in-phase pattern, a positive sloping straight line was produced; if the arms moved to the left and right at the same time, in a so-called anti-phase pattern, a negative sloping line resulted.) Two different types of feedback were compared, both of which were provided concurrently with the movement. In the "circle feedback" condition, participants were continuously shown the pattern they were creating on the screen. They were aware that the goal pattern was a circle, but they were never explicitly informed as to how to coordinate their arm movements in order to produce a circle. In the "limb feedback" condition, participants were informed about the required coordination pattern of their arms and were provided with online feedback about the position of each arm at each point in time. In addition, after every fourth trial, both groups received feedback about the actual pattern produced relative to the goal (circle) pattern. Thus, even though the two feedback conditions differed in various ways (e.g., the "complexity" of, or amount of information provided by, the feedback), the circle feedback condition could be considered an external focus condition, whereas the limb feedback condition could be considered an internal focus condition.

The results showed that circle feedback resulted in a more accurate bimanual coordination pattern than limb feedback during the practice phase, as well as on retention tests (with and without feedback). Apparently, simply providing learners with the goal pattern and with feedback about the pattern they actually produced was enough to result in the learning of the correct coordination pattern. That is, it was not necessary to inform them about how their arms needed to be coordinated to produce the pattern. In fact, instructing them and providing them feedback about the arm movement coordination pattern led to less effective performance and learning.

With the increased use of computers in areas such as second-language learning or singing training and the capability to provide the learner with on-line feedback, questions of feedback effectiveness become relevant in those areas as well. For example, a number of computer programs are now available to assist with singing training (for a review, see Hoppe, Sadakata, & Desain, 2006). These tools can provide real-time visual feedback on various aspects of performance, including pitch, timbre, shimmer, or jitter. In their review of studies that examined the usefulness of such feedback on singing performance, Hoppe et al. (2006) came to the conclusion that this type of concurrent feedback can be a quite effective addition to traditional singing lessons with a teacher. For example, they cite a study by Welch, Rush, and Howard (1989), which showed an improvement in the development of pitching ability in primary school children with real-time visual feedback (VFB), compared to a control group without VFB. Referring to the internal versus external focus differences, Hoppe et al. (2006) note that the attentional focus induced by the feedback may qualify its effectiveness: ". . . VFB that is directed to one's own movements (e.g., the vocal tract) may be less effective than VFB on the acoustical output (e.g., real-time spectral information)" (pg. 316). Hoppe and colleagues also cite some previous findings that might be accounted for by the effects of attentional focus, such as interview data in a study by Welch, Howard, Himonides, and Brereton (2005), according to which singing teachers preferred a spectrogram to all other types of feedback.

Thus, there is some evidence that the type of focus induced by concurrent feedback affects learning. Concurrent feedback, such as the feedback provided by a computer in the studies just reviewed, might be particularly relevant for training that takes place in laboratory-type settings, or for simulators that provide instantaneous information about the produced movement pattern. In most real-world settings, however, feedback is provided by instructors. In contrast to the feedback we just discussed, instructors typically provide feedback *after* the movement. In addition, they usually comment on the *quality* of the movement pattern, rather than provide quantitative information. In the next section, we will therefore look at studies that have examined how this type of feedback subsequent to the movement affects the learning of sport skills, depending on whether it tends to induce an internal or external focus of attention.

ATTENTIONAL INSIGHTS

The effects of concurrent feedback described in this section are reminiscent of some interesting results that Franz Mechsner, a former colleague of mine at the Max Planck Institute for Psychological Research in Munich, Germany, obtained in his studies on bimanual coordination (e.g., Mechsner, 2004; Mechsner et al., 2001). Mechsner's studies followed up on the well-known phenomenon that in-phase movements (e.g., those in which the two hands move in mirror symmetry) are easier to produce, especially at high frequencies, than anti-phase movements (e.g., those in which the two hands move in parallel). You can easily experience this, for example, by oscillating your index fingers in parallel. When you increase the speed of the oscillations, you will probably find that your fingers end up moving in symmetry. What Mechsner tried to show is that the preferred in-phase pattern, rather than being "hardwired," was based on the "perceptual goal" of the movement.

The way Mechsner tried to provide evidence for this idea was rather ingenious. He used a Playmobile kit (who said that scientists don't like to play?) and built an apparatus consisting of two flags that were attached to two handles via cranks. Participants, sitting at a table, moved the handles (which were positioned under the table surface so that they couldn't be seen) in circles and observed the circle movements of the flags on top of the table. In one condition, Mechsner turned one of the flags by 180°, so that an in-phase movement pattern of the hands would produce an anti-phase pattern of the flags, and vice versa. The interesting result was that, when participants started out with an anti-phase circle pattern of the flags (produced by an in-phase pattern of the hands) and then increased the speed, they tended to switch into a in-phase pattern of the flags (i.e., an anti-phase pattern of the hands)! Thus, the switch in the hand movement pattern was *opposite* to what is normally observed. Mechsner interpreted this and other related findings as evidence that actions are governed by "perceptual goals" (in this case, the perception of the flags), and that "the corresponding motor activity . . . is spontaneously and flexibly tuned in" (Mechsner et al., 2001, p. 69).

Mechsner's findings are somewhat different from those relating to the effects of external versus internal foci of attention in that performance of his task is dependent on the availability of feedback from the flags. When the flags are removed, participants are typically not able to produce the complex movement patterns they were able to produce with the flags. Yet his findings are also similar to those relating to attentional focus effects; both sets of findings show that focusing on the (perceptual) goal, or movement effect, allows the motor system to "spontaneously" produce effective movements. In fact, Mechsner and colleagues also noted, on the basis of their observations, "Anecdotal evidence seems to suggest that attention to the hands disrupts control of iso-frequency of the flags" (Mechsner et al., 2001, p. 72).

SPORT SKILL LEARNING

A few years ago, my colleagues and I conducted a study in which we compared the effectiveness of feedback that induced an external or internal focus for the learning of sport skills (Wulf et al., 2002). In one experiment, we had participants practice the volleyball "tennis" serve. In a first step, we used various volleyball textbooks to select various feedback statements. The descriptions of the technique in those textbooks basically all referred to the player's body movements. On the basis of these descriptions, we created four statements that referred to critical aspects of the technique, and we used these statements to provide participants with feedback. We labeled this type of feedback internal focus feedback. Next, we "translated" these statements into statements that contained the same information but directed the learners' attention more to the movement effects (see table 3.1). We called this type of feedback external focus feedback. For example, instead of instructing learners to shift their weight from the back leg to the front leg while hitting the ball (internal focus), we instructed them to shift their weight toward the target (external focus). After every fifth practice trial, the performer was provided with the feedback statement that was deemed most appropriate based on his or her performance on the previous five trials.

While the main purpose of this experiment was to examine whether the benefits of external versus internal focus feedback seen in our previous study (Shea & Wulf, 1999) would generalize to the learning of a sport skill, the experiment also had another purpose. We wanted to determine whether the type of feedback would have differential effects depending on the performer's level of expertise. Whereas most previous studies had used beginners without prior experience on the given task, in this study we used both novices and

TABLE 3.1   VOLLEYBALL INTERNAL AND EXTERNAL FOCUS FEEDBACK

Task type	Tennis serve	
Goal	Serve into a target area	
Feedback	**Internal focus**	**External focus**
1.	Toss the ball high enough in front of the hitting arm.	Toss the ball straight up.
2.	Snap your wrist while hitting the ball to produce a forward rotation of the ball.	Imagine holding a bowl in your hand and cupping the ball with it to produce a forward rotation of the ball.
3.	Shortly before hitting the ball, shift your weight from the back leg to the front leg.	Shortly before hitting the ball, shift your weight toward the target.
4.	Arch your back and accelerate first the shoulder, then the upper arm, then the lower arm, and finally your hand.	Hit the ball as if using a whip, like a horseman driving horses.

Reprinted, by permission, from G. Wulf et al., 2002, "Feedback and attentional focus: Enhancing the learning of sport skills through external-focus feedback," *Journal of Motor Behavior* 34: 171-182.

advanced volleyball players as participants. It seemed possible, for example, that the type of feedback would have less of an effect on advanced players, as their movements could be assumed to be more automated and therefore might be less influenced by feedback that directed their attention to their movements. Alternatively, as we saw in chapter 1, experienced performers who focus on their actions often show performance decrements. Thus, it seemed possible that advanced players and novices would be affected similarly by the type of feedback.

To measure the accuracy of the serves, we marked a target area in the center of the "opponents'" side of the court. The target was 3 × 3 m (3.3 × 3.3 yd) wide, and 4 × 4 m and 5 × 5 m areas were marked around it. If the center area was hit, 4 points were awarded. Scores of 3, 2, and 1 were awarded if one of the two larger areas or any other area on the other side of the court was hit, respectively. For balls that were out of bounds or that hit the net, 0 points were recorded.

The accuracy scores achieved by the novice and advanced groups under the two focus conditions are shown in figure 3.3. As you can see, the accuracy of the serves was greatly enhanced by external relative to internal focus feedback. This was the case not only for the

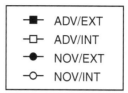

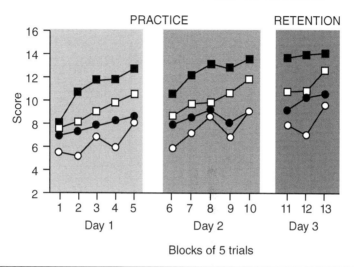

FIGURE 3.3 Accuracy scores of the advanced-external, advanced-internal, novice-external, and novice-internal groups in the volleyball study by Wulf and colleagues (2002, Experiment 1).

Reprinted, by permission, from G. Wulf et al., 2002, "Feedback and attentional focus: Enhancing the learning of sport skills through external-focus feedback," *Journal of Motor Behavior* 34: 171-182.

practice phase (when the feedback was given). Even after a one-week retention interval, in a retention test without feedback, the benefits of having received feedback that induced an external focus were still seen. Interestingly, this was true not only for novice players, but also for advanced players who already had experience with this type of serve. It should also be noted that this advantage in the movement outcome was not accomplished at the expense of movement form, which was similar for the external and internal focus groups in the study. Thus, wording feedback so that direct references to the performer's movement coordination were avoided, and attention was more directed to the movement outcome, resulted in greater accuracy of the serves.

We still wanted to replicate these findings with a different task. In addition, we wanted to have additional evidence that external focus feedback benefits learning in more advanced individuals. In a subsequent experiment, we therefore used a soccer task (Wulf et al., 2002, Experiment 2), having participants with soccer experience perform lofted passes. Participants had to shoot at a target, hung in the goal, that was 15 m (16.4 yd) away. The target was 1.4 m (1.5 yd) in height and width, and its lower edge was positioned 1 m (1 yd) above the ground. The central target area measured 80 × 80 cm (31 × 31 in.), and two zones, each 15 cm (6 in.) wide, surrounded the central area. If the ball hit the center area, 3 points were awarded. Scores of 2 or 1 were awarded if one of the larger areas was hit. As in the volleyball study, the feedback statements given to internal and external focus groups were similar in information content. However, while the internal focus statements encouraged participants to attend to their body movements, the external focus statements directed their attention more to the movement effects (see table 3.2).

Another purpose of this experiment was to see whether the frequency with which feedback was provided would differentially affect learning depending on whether it induced an internal or external focus. If so, this could have theoretical implications for how feedback "works." These will be discussed later (see section "Theoretical Implications"). In this study, we therefore gave each group feedback on either 33% or 100% of the practice trials, resulting in four groups: internal-33%, internal-100%, external-33%, and external-100%. For the two groups receiving 100% feedback, one of the five feedback statements was given after each practice trial; for the two groups receiving 33% feedback, one of these statements was provided after every third trial. The experimenter chose the statement reflecting the aspect of the skill that needed the most improvement.

Figure 3.4 shows the accuracy scores of the four groups during practice and retention. As you can see, if the feedback was phrased so as to induce an external rather than internal focus, the accuracy of the shots was significantly improved. The two external focus feedback groups (external-100%, external-33%) were overall more accurate than the two internal focus feedback groups (internal-100%, internal-33%) in retention. This is particularly interesting as the retention test was conducted one week after the practice phase, and no feedback was given on this test. Another finding is noteworthy: While the 33% group had higher accuracy scores than the 100% group under internal focus condition, the opposite was the case for the external feedback groups. Even though the two external focus groups were not statistically different from each other, the high frequency of

TABLE 3.2   SOCCER INTERNAL AND EXTERNAL FOCUS FEEDBACK

Task type	Lofted passes	
Goal	Complete lofted pass into hanging target	
Feedback	**Internal focus**	**External focus**
1.	Position your foot below the ball's midline to lift the ball.	Strike the ball below its midline to lift it; that is, kick underneath it.
2.	Position your body weight and the nonkicking foot behind the ball.	Be behind the ball, not over it, and lean back.
3.	Lock your ankle down and use the instep to strike the ball.	Stroke the ball toward the target as if passing to another player.
4.	Keep your knee bent as you swing your leg back, and straighten your knee before contact.	Use a long lever action like the swing of a golf club before contact with the ball.
5.	To strike the ball, the swing of the leg should be as long as possible.	To strike the ball, create a pendulum-like motion with as long a duration as possible.

Reprinted, by permission, from G. Wulf et al., 2002, "Feedback and attentional focus: Enhancing the learning of sport skills through external-focus feedback," *Journal of Motor Behavior* 34: 171-182.

feedback (100%) clearly did not hamper learning. However, the high feedback frequency did negatively affect learning under the internal focus condition. Our belief about why this happened and what it means for theoretical accounts of feedback are discussed next. See also "Practical Applications" on page 104.

THEORETICAL IMPLICATIONS

Both the volleyball and soccer experiments showed that participants who received feedback referring to the movement effects demonstrated more effective learning than participants who were provided with feedback about their movement patterns. This was the case for both novices and advanced performers. This finding seems to be at odds with the "guidance" hypothesis of feedback, though. According to that view, feedback is most effective if it gives the learner a chance to process the intrinsic feedback associated with the movement (e.g., Salmoni et al., 1984; Schmidt, 1991). In other

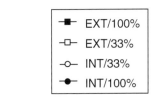

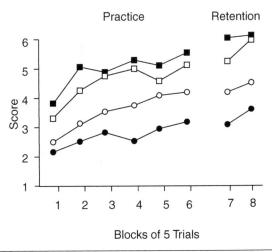

FIGURE 3.4 Accuracy of the external-100%, external-33%, internal-100%, and internal-33% groups in the soccer study by Wulf and colleagues (2002, Experiment 2).

Reprinted, by permission, from G. Wulf et al., 2002, "Feedback and attentional focus: Enhancing the learning of sport skills through external-focus feedback," *Journal of Motor Behavior* 34: 171-182.

words, feedback is assumed to be beneficial if it enhances learners' awareness of their body movements. In fact, from a guidance theory point of view, one might expect internal focus feedback to be most effective, as it encourages learners—at least on no-feedback trials—to focus on their intrinsic feedback. The results of the volleyball and soccer experiments, as well as those of the stabilometer experiment (see section "Attentional Focus and Concurrent Feedback"), clearly show that internal feedback was not more effective than external feedback, however. In fact, the opposite was the case.

The findings of the volleyball and soccer studies present several problems for the guidance view. Specifically, the guidance theory is not able to explain (a) the benefits of external relative to internal focus feedback, (b) the advantages of reduced internal focus feedback during practice (where the guidance properties of frequent feedback should facilitate performance), and (c) the interaction between feedback type and frequency. Our findings suggest not only that attentional focus is indeed an important qualifying variable for the effectiveness of feedback, but also that a fresh look at previous findings, and perhaps reinterpretation, might be required to yield a better understanding of the functions of feedback.

I would therefore like to suggest an alternative interpretation of the detrimental effects of frequent feedback found in previous studies (e.g., Lai & Shea, 1998; Weeks & Kordus, 1998; Winstein, Pohl, & Lewthwaite, 1994; Winstein & Schmidt, 1990; Wulf & Schmidt, 1989; Wulf, Schmidt, & Deubel, 1993). Rather than preventing learners from focusing on their own movements, frequent feedback might actually make them focus *too much* on their movements, leading to

© Human Kinetics

Reduced feedback effects could be due to the relief that this reduction offers from the constant internal focus induced by every-trial feedback.

the typically observed learning decrements. Reducing the relative feedback frequency, on the other hand, might give the learner a chance, at least once in a while, to perform the movement without being too concerned about his or her performance. Even though this does not necessarily induce an external focus, *not* focusing on the movement itself can be more effective than directing one's attention to one's own performance (Singer, Lidor, & Cauraugh, 1993; Wulf & Weigelt, 1997).

The assumption underlying this interpretation is that the feedback typically provided in experiments tends to induce an internal focus. Indeed, this might not be an unfair assumption. Consider, for example, the results of a study by Weeks and Kordus (1998). In that study, different groups of participants practicing a soccer throw-in were given KP, similar to the internal focus feedback given in our volleyball and soccer experiments (Wulf et al., 2002). Statements included, for example, "The feet, hips, knees, and shoulders should be aimed at the target, feet shoulder-width apart"; "The back should be arched at the beginning of the throw"; and "The arms should go over the head during the throw and finish by being aimed at the target." One of a total of eight feedback statements was given either after every trial (100%) or after every third trial (33%). The results showed a superior movement form for the 33%-KP group participants relative to the 100%-KP group participants. Interestingly, the benefits for the 33%-KP condition were seen not only in retention and transfer tests without KP, but also during practice. While the benefits of the reduced feedback condition in retention and transfer could be explained by the guidance hypothesis (e.g., Salmoni et al., 1984), the fact that these advantages were present during practice is contrary to the predictions of this view. According to the guidance hypothesis, frequent feedback would be expected to exert its strong guidance properties and lead to reduced errors when it is present during practice. However, this finding of Weeks and Kordus makes sense from an attentional focus point of view, in that the 100%-KP condition was detrimental to both practice and retention or transfer performance because of the constant internal focus it induced. The reduced feedback frequency, on the other hand, might have alleviated the negative effects of the KP because information referring to the participants' body movements was not constantly presented.

While it is relatively easy to see that KP, which by definition refers to the nature of the movement pattern, would induce an internal focus, this case might be somewhat more difficult to make for KR, which refers to the outcome of the movement in the environment (Schmidt & Lee, 2005, p. 366). One might maintain that KR about movement time, final position, or score achieved, for example, should induce more of an external focus, and therefore—according to our argument—no detrimental effects of frequent KR would be expected. On the other hand, when we look at the tasks that have been used in experiments examining KR frequency effects, it appears that the feedback was indeed very closely related to the movements that produced the outcome. For example, several studies used a movement patterning task in which a manipulandum had to be moved in a spatially and temporally defined way (e.g., Nicholson & Schmidt, 1991; Vander Linden, Cauraugh, & Greene, 1993; Winstein & Schmidt, 1990; Wrisberg & Wulf, 1997; Wulf, Schmidt, & Deubel, 1993). Obviously, the feedback in terms of the produced position–time curve presented on a screen was directly related not only to the movements of the manipulandum, but also to the limb movement. Thus, participants might have interpreted it as representing their arm movement, that is, as internal focus feedback (or KP). This also holds for positioning tasks (e.g., Winstein, Pohl, & Lewthwaite, 1994), in which a lever has to be moved to a certain target position in a specified movement time. Other studies have used sequential key press tasks, in which a series of keys has to be depressed in specified movement times (e.g., Lai & Shea, 1998; Wulf, Lee, & Schmidt, 1994, Wulf & Schmidt, 1989). With the spatial accuracy demands being relatively minor in these cases, feedback about the movement times between key presses was again directly related to the finger movements.

I do not wish to discount the credibility of the guidance hypothesis. In fact, it is very likely that for typical laboratory tasks, where participants are often deprived of natural sources of feedback so that various manipulations of experimenter-provided feedback can be examined, individuals develop the dependency on the augmented feedback postulated by the guidance hypothesis if feedback is provided too frequently. That is, independent of whether the feedback induces an external or internal focus, detrimental effects of frequent feedback might be observed under such "artificial" laboratory conditions. On the other hand, under more "natural" conditions in which other sources of information are available and the development of a dependency on augmented feedback might be less likely (Wulf & Shea, 2002, 2004), the focus of attention induced by the augmented feedback might have a greater impact. Clearly, future studies need to verify (or refute) these assumptions.

SUMMARY

Even though studies on the effectiveness of feedback as a function of attentional focus are relatively scarce, it seems safe to conclude that feedback directing attention to the effects of a person's movements results in more effective learning than feedback directed at the movements per se. An external attentional focus can be achieved, for example, through a display of (concurrent) augmented kinematic or kinetic information or by the appropriate wording of feedback. At least when it comes to complex skill learning, concurrent augmented feedback given in addition to the individual's intrinsic (visual, auditory, kinesthetic, etc.) feedback does not seem to create a dependency. Also, a high frequency of verbal feedback given after the completion of the movement does not appear to be detrimental, provided that it induces an external focus. Importantly, beneficial effects of external focus feedback are seen even in delayed retention tests when the feedback is withdrawn, suggesting that those effects are relatively permanent.

PRACTICAL APPLICATIONS

WORDING FEEDBACK

Based on the findings discussed in this chapter (as well as those related to instructions discussed in chapter 2), one recommendation for applied situations seems clear: Wording feedback so that it promotes an external focus should lead to more effective performance and learning than feedback that directs attention to the coordination of the individual's body movements. For example, attention could be directed to the motion of an implement (e.g., golf club, baseball bat, badminton racket), the spin or trajectory of a ball (e.g., table tennis ball, football, soccer ball), or the amount of force exerted against an object (e.g., pole used in pole-vaulting, springboard, punching bag). Not only novices, but even advanced performers, appear to benefit from feedback inducing an external focus. (For a discussion of expertise and attentional focus effects, see chapter 5.)

- Pick a motor skill from sport and think about how "traditional" feedback (that induces an internal focus) can be reworded so that it promotes an external focus.

- How could a physical therapist or a music teacher apply these findings?

CONCURRENT FEEDBACK

Although concurrent feedback—for example, about movement kinematics or forces produced—may not be very common in applied settings, simulators are sometimes used to provide this information. For example, golf simulators can instantaneously display a performer's weight shift during the swing, and rowing simulators provide concurrent feedback about the forces exerted on each oar. Furthermore, concurrent auditory feedback can be used to provide information about certain aspects of a skill, such as the double-support phase in racewalking. Provided that the concurrent feedback is not too distracting and does not cause an information overload, it might be beneficial for learning if it directs attention away from the performer's own movements and serves to induce an external focus.

- Can you think of a real-life skill for which concurrent feedback might benefit learning?
- What might be preconditions in order for concurrent feedback to provide a learning advantage? Are there situations in which you would expect concurrent feedback to be effective, or not effective?

FEEDBACK FREQUENCY

In contrast to feedback that is directed at the coordination of the performer's movements, a high frequency of feedback does not seem to be harmful to learning if the feedback induces an external focus. In fact, relatively frequent reminders of what to focus on might prevent learners from focusing too much on their own movements, perhaps enhancing learning compared to less frequent feedback.

- How can this be tested experimentally? Can you think of a way to examine the validity of this assumption in an experiment?
- Would you expect the influence of the frequency of (internal or external focus) feedback to interact with the performer's level of expertise? If so, how?

FUTURE DIRECTIONS

FEEDBACK FREQUENCY

As of yet, only one study has addressed the interaction of feedback frequency and attentional focus (Wulf et al., 2002, Experiment 2). It would be desirable to have more evidence for the assumption that frequent feedback is detrimental only if it induces an internal focus, not if it directs the performer's attention externally. Further studies are needed to replicate and extend the findings with different tasks.

Focusing on the movement effect has several benefits.

CHAPTER 4

ADVANTAGES OF ATTENTIONAL FOCUS ON THE MOVEMENT EFFECT

A tennis player, who has been playing for a number of years but isn't very happy with the consistency of her strokes, has been experimenting with different attentional foci. She not only notices that when she focuses on producing a certain ball trajectory, rather than on how she executes the swing, her strokes are more accurate and reliable; she also makes the observation that she feels more "relaxed." She can direct more attention to her strategy, and she doesn't seem to get tired as quickly, either mentally or physically.

What exactly is it about our focus of attention that affects our performance, as well as our learning of motor skills? What happens when we focus on the execution of our movements? Why do we perform more effectively and learn faster when we focus on the outcome, or effect, of our movements? Or, is it perhaps sufficient *not* to focus on our movements? Is focusing on the movement effect beneficial simply because it prevents individuals from focusing on their movements? Thus it is important to ask the question: Is it actually necessary to focus on the movement *effect*, or is *any* "external" focus beneficial? If it is critical that we focus on something that is outside of (i.e., external to) our body, it might be irrelevant whether we concentrate, for example, on the tennis ball trajectory we are trying to produce (a movement effect) or on the net (not a movement effect). Alternatively, there might be something special about focusing on the movement effect. Perhaps it somehow "triggers" the actions necessary to produce the effect. These are the issues considered in this chapter. We will see how focusing on the movement effect influences the control of our movements and leads to the learning advantages discussed in the previous two chapters. A few studies have not shown the "typical" benefits of an external compared to an internal (or no) focus, or the differences were not as clear as one might have expected. At the end of the chapter, therefore, we will discuss what seem to be preconditions for attentional focus effects to occur.

FOCUSING ON THE MOVEMENT EFFECT

As we discussed in chapter 1, some scientists believe that it is important *not* to think about the movement while executing it (e.g., Masters, 1992; Maxwell, Masters, & Eves, 2000; Singer, 1985, 1988). For example, Singer suggested that the performer go though the motion mentally *before* actually performing the movement (step 2 of his Five-Step Approach). Subsequently, the performer is supposed to direct attention to an external cue in order to block out other thoughts; and during movement execution, the performer is instructed not to think about anything. Masters (1992) contends that conscious thought processes should be avoided altogether. Therefore, learners should be given as little instruction as possible. Otherwise, they may try to apply this knowledge and adopt a conscious mode of control, which is assumed to interfere with the automatic execution of the movement. For this reason, in their studies Masters and colleagues

Is not focusing on anything as effective as focusing on the swing of the club?
Photo courtesy of Mathew and Brady Byers.

often have learners perform secondary tasks, such as random letter generation or tone counting, while practicing a motor skill (e.g., Masters, 1992; Maxwell, Masters, & Eves, 2000). This way, rules or explicit knowledge regarding the skill—which learners might develop if they were not distracted—is supposed to be reduced to a minimum.

Is it possible that the main advantage of adopting an external focus is that attention is not directed to the actual movement? In other words, is the only function of focusing on the movement effect that it blocks out other thoughts, or that it prevents individuals from gaining explicit knowledge about the movement? If this were the case, preventing learners from focusing on their movements by having them perform an attention-demanding secondary task might be just as effective as instructing them to focus on the movement effect. Yet, if there is an advantage to focusing on the movement effect, relative to focusing on another task, the former condition should lead to more effective learning.

Nancy McNevin and I examined this question (Wulf & McNevin, 2003) in a study in which we had participants learn the stabilometer task. One of the practice conditions was designed to prevent learners from focusing on their actions. In this condition, participants were required to continuously shadow, that is, repeat out loud, a story presented to them via a tape recorder while they were balancing on the stabilometer. Shadowing is a rather demanding task, so participants were not able to devote a great deal of attention, if any, to the balance task. We compared the effectiveness of the shadowing condition to that of external and internal focus conditions similar to those used in our previous studies. In the external focus group, participants were instructed to focus on keeping markers on the stabilometer platform horizontal, whereas in the internal focus group they were instructed to focus on keeping their feet horizontal. In addition, we included a control group without any attentional focus instructions.

The results are shown in figure 4.1. A couple of things are noteworthy here. First, the external focus condition was more effective than the shadowing condition. This was the case not only for performance during practice, when one might expect the secondary task requirement to degrade balance performance. Rather, the shadowing group was also less effective than the external focus group during retention, when the shadowing task was removed. This suggests that there were no "hidden" learning advantages of having to perform a distracting task. These results indicate that there is, in fact, an advantage to focusing on the movement effect. Simply "distracting" learners was not enough. Second, the external focus advantage was seen not only in relation to the shadowing group, but also in relation to the internal focus and control groups. As you can see from figure 4.1, there was no difference between the internal focus and control groups in the retention test. This finding is similar to the results of the ski simulator experiment discussed earlier (Wulf, Höß, & Prinz, 1998, Experiment 2). Those findings showed that instructions referring to the actual body movements are rather ineffective—in fact, no more effective than no instructions at all. The important point is that distracting learners from the motor task to be learned was not very effective. Even though it was not detrimental, it clearly didn't benefit learning. In contrast, having learners focus on the movement effect did.

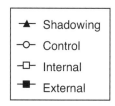

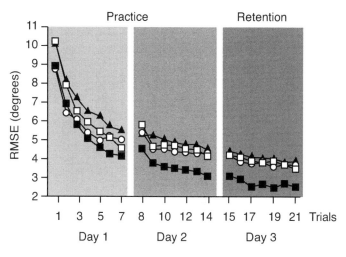

FIGURE 4.1 Deviations of the stabilometer platform from the horizontal (root-mean-square error) for the internal focus, external focus, shadowing, and control groups in the study by Wulf and McNevin (2003).

Reprinted, by permission, from G. Wulf and N.H. McNevin, 2003, "Simply distracting learners is not enough: More evidence for the learning benefits of an external focus of attention," *European Journal of Sport Science* 3(5): 1-13.

One question remains, however: Is there an advantage to focusing on the movement effect, or is it simply important to focus attention on a *skill-related* external cue, such as the golf ball you are about to hit? Remember, the main purpose of external cues used in Singer's Five-Step Approach (e.g., Singer, 1985, 1988) is to prevent the learner from focusing on the details of movement coordination while he or she is executing the skill. If it suffices to focus on a skill-related external cue, it shouldn't matter whether a tennis player focuses, for example, on the approaching ball or on the (anticipated) trajectory of the ball she or he is hitting. Both are external cues and both are skill related, but only the latter represents a movement effect. If it is more effective to focus on the movement effect, a focus on the anticipated ball trajectory should result in better performance.

My colleagues and I examined exactly this question a few years ago (Wulf et al., 2000). In our study, novice tennis players practiced the tennis forehand stroke. We first gave them basic instructions regarding the correct technique of the forehand stroke, and then we asked them to hit tennis balls to a target on the other side of the court. One group of participants was instructed to focus on the ball approaching them, or the "antecedent" of their action. We therefore called this group the antecedent group. Another group was instructed to focus on the ball leaving their racket. We called this group the effect group. Thus, participants in both groups adopted an "external" focus of attention by focusing on the ball, but only participants in the latter group directed their attention to the movement effect. One day after the practice phase we conducted a retention test, as we wanted to see whether the type of focus had an influence on learning. As usual, we did not give participants attentional focus instructions or reminders on this second day.

The results provided support for the idea that there is indeed an advantage to focusing on the movement effect (see figure 4.2). Even though there were no differences between groups during practice, the retention test results showed that those participants who focused on the effect of their movements (i.e., the anticipated trajectory of the ball leaving the racket) were superior to participants who focused on the antecedent (i.e., the trajectory of the approaching ball). Thus, focusing on the movement effect was more effective for learning than directing attention to another external cue. This suggests that the critical issue is not the "external" focus per se, but that attention is directed to the effect of the movement.

Of course, this raises the question of what exactly it is about the movement effect that benefits learning. What happens when we direct our attention to the movement effect instead of to the movements themselves (or something else)? How does the control of our movements change? How is it possible that, when we simply concentrate on the movement effect, or desired outcome, our actions suddenly become more effective?

CONSTRAINED ACTION HYPOTHESIS

To explain the advantages of an (effect related) external focus of attention, my colleagues and I have proposed the *constrained action hypothesis* (e.g., McNevin, Shea, & Wulf, 2003; Wulf, McNevin, & Shea, 2001; Wulf, Shea, & Park, 2001). Charlie Shea was particularly instrumental in formulating these ideas. He also suggested a special type of move-

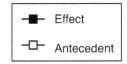

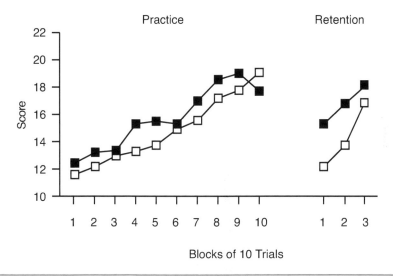

FIGURE 4.2 Accuracy scores of the effect and antecedent groups in the tennis study by Wulf and colleagues (2000, Experiment 1). Higher scores indicate greater accuracy.

ment analysis (fast Fourier transform; see later) to test these ideas. Essentially, the constrained action view suggests that when individuals focus on their movements (i.e., adopt an internal attentional focus), they tend to consciously intervene in control processes that regulate the coordination of their movements. Yet, by attempting to actively control their movements, they inadvertently disrupt automatic processes that have the capacity to control movements effectively and efficiently. In contrast, focusing attention on the movement effect promotes a more automatic type of control. It allows unconscious, fast, and reflexive processes to control the movements, with the result that the desired outcome is achieved almost as a by-product. In other words, adopting an external focus reduces conscious interference in the processes that control our movements and, as a consequence, results in enhanced performance and learning.

Constrained Action Hypothesis

➤ Focusing on one's movements (i.e., adopting an *internal focus*) constitutes a conscious intervention into control processes that would "normally" regulate movements effectively and efficiently. That is, trying to actively control those movements disrupts automatic control processes.

➤ Focusing on the movement effect (i.e., adopting an *external focus*) promotes a more automatic type of control. It takes advantage of unconscious and reflexive processes and allows them to control our movements to a greater extent. As a result, performance and learning are enhanced.

This may remind you of the stages of learning that we talked about in chapter 1. People typically adopt an internal focus early in the learning process, when they tend to direct attention to the coordination of the various movements (or submovements) that constitute the skill. There could be several reasons for this tendency to control movements in a relatively conscious manner. For example, individuals who have little or no experience with a given skill tend to be insecure; and, through conscious control attempts, they try to ensure that they perform the movement correctly. In addition, the instructions given to them might promote this type of attentional focus. Also, if there is a risk of falling, people are likely to be extra cautious; and by "freezing" the degrees of freedom of the motor system or stiffening their limbs, they try to reduce this risk. Finally, most people intuitively believe that conscious control of one's movements is necessary when one is first acquiring a motor skill. In fact, as we have seen, many scientists share this belief (e.g., Beilock & Carr, 2004; Meinel & Schnabel, 1976). With practice and experience, of course, our movements are usually controlled with an increasing degree of automaticity.

How can an external focus promote automaticity if we have never or rarely performed a particular skill before? Even though we might never have performed the given skill before, we might have had experience with similar skills. For example, almost everybody has extensive experience standing upright. Over most of our lifetime, our postural system has learned to make automatic adjustments that prevent us from losing our balance. If we were required to stand on a compliant, or even a moving, support surface, we would still be able to use some of the same control mechanisms. The same is true for more dynamic balance tasks. If you know how to do in-line skating, it might not be too difficult for you to learn ice-skating. These skills have components in common that can be transferred from one to the other. If you are fairly proficient at in-line skating and are able to perform this skill at a relatively automatic level, you would probably also be able to use some of those control processes when learning to ice-skate. In other cases, you might have performed components of a novel skill in the context of another skill. For example, experience with throwing and catching balls might transfer to juggling, so this part of the skill should be performed more or less automatically. Nevertheless, people often tend to choose a more conscious mode

© Photodisc

Even though you might never have snowboarded before, if you were a proficient skateboarder certain skills should not require much conscious control and you should be able to perform these components of snowboarding relatively automatically.

of control when confronted with new tasks. Findings showing no performance differences between participants instructed to adopt an internal focus and those with no focus instructions (e.g., Wulf, Höβ, & Prinz, 1998, Experiment 1; Wulf & McNevin, 2003; Wulf et al., 2003, Experiment 2) suggest that people might spontaneously try to control their movements in a relatively conscious manner—thereby constraining their motor system. In other words, they don't necessarily use the automatic control capabilities that they have available.

What evidence do we have for the view that an external focus results in a more automatic type of control than an internal focus, as predicted by the constrained action hypothesis? As of now, there are at least three types of evidence for this notion. The first line of evidence comes from frequency analyses of movement adjustments, particularly with regard to balance control. The findings indicate that when individuals adopt an external focus, they use faster and more automatic control processes compared to when they adopt an internal focus. The second piece of evidence is based on findings showing differences in the amount of attentional capacity required under external versus internal focus conditions. Finally, there are studies demonstrating that muscular activity is modified as a function of attentional focus. Specifically, an external focus has been shown to reduce muscular activity, thereby enhancing movement efficiency. Moreover, an external focus seems to result in more effective coordination between agonist and antagonist muscle groups than internal focus or control conditions. These findings are described in more detail next.

FREQUENCY OF MOVEMENT ADJUSTMENTS

When one observes participants on the stabilometer (see the photo on p. 40) who were instructed to focus on the markers (external focus), after some practice they appear to move the platform more smoothly than participants instructed to focus on their feet (internal focus). This observation suggests that there may be subtle differences in how individuals control their movements when they adopt different attentional foci. It turns out that this is indeed the case. When we try to stand still—especially on an unstable surface, but even during quiet standing—we constantly make small adjustments that enable us to remain in balance. As you will remember, the goal of the stabilometer task is the keep the platform in a horizontal position, or at least as close to horizontal as possible. To achieve this goal, continuous corrections of smaller or larger deviations from the horizontal are necessary. The faster the corrections are, the smaller the deviations of the platform from the horizontal. High-frequency corrections and the resulting small movement amplitudes, or platform deviations, give the appearance of relatively smooth movements, while the lower-frequency changes and correspondingly higher amplitudes result in more abrupt changes in the platform position. Do participants who adopt an external focus really make faster corrections than those with an internal focus? And, if so, what is the basis for these fast movement adjustments?

Generally, high-frequency movement adjustments are viewed as representing the incorporation and coordination of additional available degrees of freedom (Thompson & Stewart, 1986), which are typically associated with skilled performance. Consider, for example, the tremor in your hand and fingers when you are pointing at something. In young, healthy people, this tremor is almost imperceptible because the frequency of adjustments is very high. As a consequence, the amplitudes of those movements are small. This is different in motor systems that are compromised by disease (e.g., Parkinson's disease) or aging. Compromised systems often show low-frequency adjustments with large amplitudes (e.g., Gantert, Honerkamp, & Timmer, 1992; Newell, Gao, & Sprague, 1995). Higher-frequency adjustments allow the motor system to quickly respond to perturbations—be they perturbations that we produce through our own actions or perturbations from the environment.

The frequency characteristics of balance movements can be determined through use of a method known as fast Fourier transform (FFT). The FFT decomposes complex sinusoidal waveforms produced by oscillating segments (e.g., legs or arms) into simple waveforms according to their relative contribution to the overall pattern. The result of the transform will produce the dominant frequency component of the pattern, which sheds light on how the motor output was controlled. For example, if the dominant frequency is in the higher range (e.g., 6 Hz), this indicates a fairly "stiff" degree of control over the muscles or joints involved in producing the movement. However, if the dominant frequency is in the lower range (e.g., 2 Hz), it indicates a fairly loose degree of control. Generalizing this description to postural adjustments, a higher-frequency output would suggest smaller and more rapid adjustments to disturbances to balance, while a lower-frequency output would suggest larger and much slower adjustments.

Analyses of movement adjustments produced by performers adopting an internal versus external focus provide insight into the control processes that they utilize under different attentional focus conditions. Using FFT analysis, we found that people who focus on keeping the markers in front of their feet horizontal indeed make more and smaller corrections in maintaining their balance than people who focus on keeping their feet horizontal (McNevin, Shea, & Wulf, 2003; Wulf, McNevin, & Shea, 2001; Wulf, Shea, & Park, 2001). That is, participants with an external focus exhibit higher-frequency and lower-amplitude movements than those with an internal focus. What does this mean? It suggests that an external focus promotes the utilization of more (and faster) reflex loops, which operate at an automatic or unconscious level, whereas a focus on specific body movements results in the use of conscious, and therefore slower, feedback loops.

In the study of the distance effect described in chapter 2 (McNevin, Shea, & Wulf, 2003; see section "Distance Effects"), we wanted to see whether placing the markers (on which participants were focusing) at a greater distance from the feet (see figure 2.8) would lead to even higher frequencies in responding than placing markers directly in front of the feet. This is indeed what we found. First, as can be seen in figure 4.3, participants instructed to focus on their feet (internal) had generally lower mean power frequency (MPF) values than the external focus groups (near, far outside, far inside). Second, and more importantly, the two groups that focused on the distant markers (far outside, far inside) made more and smaller corrections than the group that focused on the markers close to the feet (near). Thus, focusing on the more remote movement effects resulted in higher frequencies of responding than focusing on effects closer to the body or adopting an internal focus. This suggests that balance control was even more automatic when individuals focused on an effect that was farther away from the body—and thus more easily distinguishable from the body movements that produced the effect.

These findings were a first piece of evidence that internal versus external attentional foci result in the utilization of different control processes. If an external focus of attention indeed promotes the use of more automatic motor control processes, performance should also require less attentional capacity compared to an internal focus, whereby information is processed at a more conscious level. We tested this prediction in another experiment that is described in the next section.

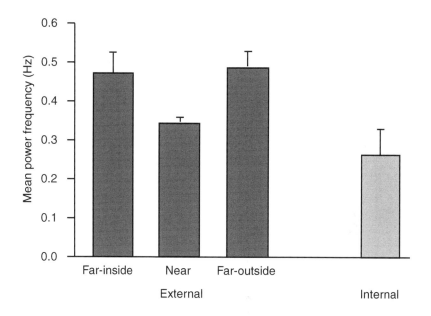

FIGURE 4.3 Mean power frequency for the internal, far-outside, near, and far-inside conditions (McNevin, Shea, & Wulf, 2003).

Reprinted, by permission, from G. Wulf and N.H. McNevin, 2003, "Simply distracting learners is not enough: More evidence for the learning benefits of an external focus of attention," *European Journal of Sport Science* 3(5): 1-13.

DIFFERENCES IN ATTENTIONAL DEMANDS

To determine the attentional demands of a particular task, psychologists often use probe reaction time (RT) tasks. In this paradigm, participants who are performing a (primary) task simultaneously have to perform a (secondary) probe RT task, such as pressing a button as quickly as possible in response to a visual or auditory signal. Performance on the probe RT task is assumed to be related to the attentional demands of the primary task. That is, longer reaction times are interpreted as indicating that the primary task required more attention (e.g., Abernethy, 1988).

In one study, we used this dual-task procedure to assess the attentional demands associated with internal and external foci of attention (Wulf, McNevin, & Shea, 2001). We wanted to see whether performing a motor task with an external, as compared to an internal, focus indeed required less attentional capacity. While performing the stabilometer task, participants under external (focus on markers on the platform) and internal (focus on feet) conditions were asked to hold a response key and to respond as fast as possible with a finger press to randomly presented tones. We predicted that, if an external attentional focus results in a more automatic type of control than an internal focus, less attentional capacity should be required; and, because the remaining (larger) attentional capacity could be dedicated to the RT task, faster probe RTs should be the consequence.

The results of the experiment confirmed this prediction. First, probe RTs became shorter across practice trials for both groups, indicating that with more experience, less attention was required to balance on the stabilometer. Second, and more importantly, probe RTs for the external focus group were generally lower throughout practice and retention relative to those for the internal focus group. This corroborates the view that the adoption of an external focus prompts greater automaticity and thus provides another piece of evidence for the constrained action view.

MUSCULAR ACTIVITY

As we saw in the previous two chapters, the adoption of an external compared to an internal focus results in differences at the behavioral level: An external focus typically leads to more effective performance, such as better balance or greater accuracy in golf, soccer, tennis, or basketball shots. How exactly does this come about? Are there correlates at a neuromuscular level that can explain the performance differences seen under external versus internal focus conditions? One way to more gain insight into how the nervous system operates to produce attentional focus effects is to look at muscular activity. Electromyography (EMG) allows researchers to determine, for example, how much muscular activity is produced under each focus condition. If, as proposed by the constrained action hypothesis, an external focus results in greater automaticity than an internal focus, one might expect to see more discriminate motor unit recruitment under external relative to internal focus conditions. That is, an external focus should result in *more efficient* movements.

In order to understand how an external focus would produce a more economical movement pattern, keep in mind that our body is an energy-efficient system that tries to conserve energy. For example, if it were possible to pick up an object by using a single motor unit (i.e., a motor neuron and the muscle fibers it innervates), our body would do this, rather than use two motor units and waste energy. With regard to postural control, for instance, our body tries to minimize sway, because bringing its center of gravity back to a central position would require more energy if the deviations from this central position were greater. One of the predictions we made was that an external focus would exploit the energy-conserving nature of the body. For a motor system to exploit these energy-conserving characteristics, the system has to be sensitive to the movement effects it produces (McNevin & Wulf, 2002). If attention is directed to the effect, or outcome, of an action—as it is when an external focus is adopted—there should be a greater coherence between the outcome and the sensory consequences of that action. This greater sensory-motor coherence allows the motor system to adjust more adaptively to task demands. As a result, only the minimally necessary number of motor units required to produce a desired outcome would be recruited.

In our first study examining muscular activity as a function of attentional focus, we had participants perform biceps curls under either internal or external focus conditions (Vance et al., 2004). All participants performed under both conditions, and all performed two sets of 10 repetitions under each condition. Half of the participants first performed one set with an internal focus and then performed the next set with an external focus, and so forth, while the other half started with an external focus. Under the internal focus condition, participants were instructed to concentrate on their arms while lifting the weight, whereas under the external focus condition they were instructed to focus on the curl bar. We measured EMG activities of the biceps and triceps brachii muscles during the curls. If those movements are controlled more automatically and more efficiently with an external focus, one should see less EMG activity with an external compared to an internal focus.

While the results were generally in line with our expectation, one finding was somewhat unexpected: The biceps curls were executed faster under the external focus condition, even though movement speed was not an explicit goal of the task. Yet the fact that movements were spontaneously performed more rapidly when participants focused on the curl bar, rather than their arms, is in accordance with the automaticity notion: A more automatic mode of control typically results in more fluid and smoother movements, which in turn might lead to a faster movement execution.

Figure 4.4 shows integrated EMG (iEMG) activity for the biceps and triceps muscles during the two sets of repetitions under each focus condition. Integrated EMG activity reflects the combined influence of the temporal (movement time) and spatial (EMG ampli-

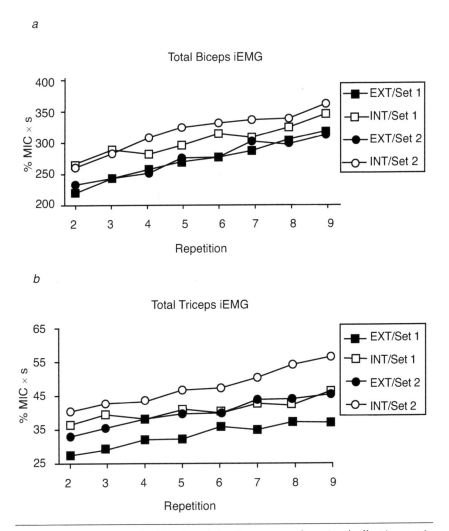

FIGURE 4.4 Integrated EMG activity (in percent of maximal-effort isometric contraction [MIC] × s) of the (a) biceps and (b) triceps muscles during biceps curls in the study by Vance and colleagues (2004). (Only repetitions 2-9 are shown because the first and last repetition in each condition were mechanically different, as they started from, and ended in, a stopped position, respectively.)

Adapted, by permission, from J. Vance et al., 2004, "EMG activity as a function of the performer's focus of attention," Journal of Motor Behavior 36: 450-459.

tude) characteristics of muscle activity. As you can see from the figure, muscle activity generally increased across repetitions and, at least for the triceps, also from the first to the second set. That is, with increasing fatigue, more muscular activity was required to lift the weight. Interestingly, though, muscular activity was generally lower when individuals adopted an external relative to an internal focus. As the movement outcome (weight lifted) was identical under the two conditions, this indicates that movements were produced with less energy, or greater efficiency, when an external focus was adopted. Note also that the external focus resulted in reduced iEMG activity not only of the biceps muscles (i.e., the agonists), but also of the triceps muscles (i.e., the antagonists). Of course, the triceps counteracts the biceps; therefore, its activity should be as low as possible to facilitate the effectiveness and efficiency of biceps activity. It is interesting to see that this was achieved to a greater extent with an external focus, as it seems to suggest that movement economy was enhanced, at least in part, through a more effective coordination between agonist and antagonist muscle groups.

Even though the results of this experiment appeared to corroborate the constrained action notion, one has to take into account that iEMG activity is a function of movement time. That is, there was a possibility that the reduced iEMG activity under the external focus condition was due to the fact that the curls were produced faster. We felt that the support would be even stronger if differences in EMG activity were not mediated by differences in movement time. Therefore, we conducted a follow-up experiment in which we used a metronome and required participants to perform their movements in synchrony with the clicks produced by the metronome (Vance et al., 2004, Experiment 2). The results of that experiment produced even stronger support for the constrained action notion: Even though the curls were executed with the same speed under both conditions, muscular activity of the biceps muscles was reduced when individuals focused on the bar while lifting the weight compared to when they focused on their arms. There was also less triceps activity under the external focus condition, at least in the flexion phase. Thus, the adoption of an external focus indeed resulted in greater movement efficiency.

David Marchant and his colleagues (2006) at the University of Hull (United Kingdom) tried to replicate these findings, and they made two interesting changes to the experimental design. First, rather than using a metronome, which places additional attentional demands upon participants and might cause interference with the internal or external focus instructions, they controlled movement time by using a Biodex system, whereby movement speed is standardized throughout each repetition. Second, a control condition was added to examine whether external focus instructions might increase movement efficiency not only compared to internal focus instructions, but also compared to a "natural" control condition. This is interesting, because for a "simple" weightlifting task like biceps curls, one might not necessarily expect to find an improvement in performance just by changing the focus of attention relative to what the performer normally does. Marchant and colleagues (2006) found that instructing participants to focus on the movement of the weight bar (external focus) resulted in significantly less iEMG and peak EMG activity than either instructions to focus on their arms (internal focus) or no focus instructions (control). Thus, these findings nicely replicated and extended those of Vance and colleagues (2004). It is particularly interesting to see that the external focus instructions were able to reduce muscular activity even compared to the natural control condition.

In a more recent study, we were able to replicate these results with a different task. The biceps curl task used in the previous study did not have an "outcome" that would allow us to describe performance as more or less effective. Tiffany Zachry therefore did a study in which she examined whether external–internal focus differences in EMG activity would also be found for tasks that have a clear goal and measurable outcome, such as movement accuracy relative to the goal (Zachry et al., 2005). If differences in muscular activity were found for those tasks as well, such a result might shed more light on the mechanisms responsible for external focus advantages in movement outcome. Zachry had participants shoot basketball free throws under either external focus (focus on the rim of the basket) or internal focus (focus on wrist flexion) conditions.

Not only was shooting accuracy greater with an external focus, but EMG activity in the biceps and triceps muscles was also reduced compared to that with an internal focus. These results are interesting for a couple of reasons. First, they show that the reduced EMG activity observed under the external focus condition was accompanied by greater movement accuracy. While other studies have shown external focus advantages in movement accuracy, for example in golf shots (Wulf, Lauterbach, & Toole, 1999), volleyball serves (Wulf et al., 2002, Experiment 1), or soccer kicks (Wulf et al., 2002,

Experiment 2; Wulf, Wächter, & Wortmann, 2003), this study was the first to demonstrate both an increase in movement accuracy *and* a reduction in muscular activity with an external focus. This result seems to suggest that a greater level of "noise" in the motor system (i.e., increased EMG activity) resulting from an internal focus might hamper fine movement control and make the outcome less reliable, compared to an external focus.

Moreover, it is interesting that attentional focus differences in EMG occurred in muscle groups that participants were not specifically instructed to focus on. In the internal focus condition, they were instructed to focus on their wrist flexion. Yet while there was a trend for greater activity in the flexor carpi radialis (which is responsible for wrist flexion), significantly greater muscular activity occurred in the biceps and triceps brachii under the internal compared to the external focus condition. This suggests that the effects of attentional focus on the motor system might be rather general in that they "spread" to muscle groups that are not within the performer's focus of attention. Thus, the focus on a certain part of the body has an influence not only on the control of that part, but also on the control of other parts of the motor system. In other words, an internal focus appears to constrain not only the action of the body part that the individual focuses on, but also the action of other parts—and perhaps even the whole motor system.

ATTENTIONAL FOCUS AND THE STAGES OF LEARNING

In the first chapter, we considered the stages of learning, and we saw how the control of movements is generally assumed to shift from conscious to more automatic control as an individual practices and gains experience with a particular skill. An external focus promotes automaticity, whereas an internal focus tends to induce a more conscious type of control (and constrains the motor system). That is, when the learner adopts an external as opposed to an internal focus, it appears that the learning process is sped up and a state of automaticity is achieved sooner. Thus, one might argue that the length of the first stages of learning is shortened by the adoption of an external focus. This is illustrated in table 4.1. The table shows how the length of the learning stages—as well as the degree of conscious (dark top of arrow) versus automatic (light bottom of arrow) control—might vary, depending on the learner's focus of attention.

TABLE 4.1 STAGES OF LEARNING AS A FUNCTION OF THE ATTENTIONAL FOCUS ADOPTED BY THE LEARNER

	Stage	Internal focus	External focus
Time	Cognitive (verbal)	Large parts of the movement are controlled consciously.	Large parts of the movement are controlled consciously.
	Associative	Some parts of the movement are controlled consciously, some automatically.	Some parts of the movement are controlled consciously, some automatically.
	Autonomous (motor)	Movement is largely controlled automatically.	Movement is largely controlled automatically.

How does the learner's focus of attention relate to the stages of learning?

PRECONDITIONS FOR EXTERNAL FOCUS BENEFITS

While the research studies described in the last two chapters have demonstrated clear advantages of adopting an external focus, relative to an internal or no particular focus, a few studies did not show this pattern of results. In some cases, the reason could be confounds in the design. For example, if the instructions given under internal and external focus conditions referred to different aspects of the task, or if the instructions were so vague that we can't be sure what participants focused on (e.g., Canning, 2005; Perkins-Ceccato, Passmore, & Lee, 2003), this might well explain the failure to replicate previous results. However, there are some other factors that seem to have an influence on whether inducing an external focus through instruction or feedback "works" or not. These are the difficulty of the task and the complexity of the instructions. Let's take a look at what effects these variables have and how they might act to qualify the attentional focus effect.

TASK DIFFICULTY

Most studies on the effects of attentional focus have used relatively difficult skills that challenged participants. Those studies have consistently shown that instructions or feedback inducing an external focus are more effective than those inducing an internal or no particular focus (see chapters 2 and 3). However, a few studies have not shown those effects or have shown them only under certain conditions. What these studies seem to have in common is that the tasks were not particularly challenging for the performer. For example, in a study that is described in more detail in chapter 7, external focus instructions enhanced balance in persons with Parkinson's disease only on the most difficult of three balance tasks (Landers et al., 2005). Moreover, the external focus benefits were found only for those participants who had a history of falls—for whom the task was very challenging—whereas no significant benefits were found for those without a fall history. In another study (Wulf, Landers, & Töllner, 2006), balance on an unstable surface was enhanced through external focus instructions in older persons with Parkinson's disease, but not in young, unimpaired participants (see also chapter 5). Using a golf putting task, Lesley Tranter (2001) in my lab in Reading, United

Kingdom, did not find differences between groups of novices who were instructed to focus on their hands (internal focus) or the putter (external focus). Even though putting is not an "easy" task, it does not require complex coordination patterns between various parts of the body. Poolton and colleagues (2006), who also used a golf putting task as well as similar instructions, also did not find group differences in retention tests. However, the external focus group in that study did show more effective putting performance than the internal focus group on a transfer test. This test was more demanding than the retention test, because participants had to listen to low- and high-pitched tones presented to them while putting and were asked to count the number of high-pitched tones. (Often transfer tests are more sensitive than retention tests, presumably because they require performance under novel conditions and are therefore more challenging, and they sometimes show group differences even when retention tests do not.)

In one study, we directly examined the idea that a certain level of task difficulty is necessary for attentional focus effects to occur (Wulf, Töllner, & Shea, in press). This seemed to be important not only for theoretical reasons, but also for practical reasons, because identifying conditions that are amenable to attentional focus effects should help teachers, coaches, and therapists to utilize attentional focus instructions appropriately. On the basis of the constrained action hypothesis, it made sense to assume that attentional focus effects would occur only if the task was relatively difficult for the performer. When a motor task is difficult, directing attention to the movement effect might encourage the performer to use "motor programs" (i.e., memory representations that control an action automatically) that he or she has developed through practice with other, similar tasks. However, if the task is relatively easy and is already controlled automatically, one would not expect to find additional benefits of inducing an external focus.

In our study (Wulf, Töllner, & Shea, in press), we asked participants to stand as still as possible, and we systematically varied the stability of the surface they were standing on. In our first experiment, participants (young, healthy adults) were required to stand either on the flat metal surface of a force platform or on a foam mat placed on top of the force platform. While the foam surface was, of course, slightly less stable than the metal surface, we considered both conditions to be relatively easy. In our second experiment, we chose two tasks that were more challenging. Both involved balancing on an inflated rubber disk. Standing on the disk results in less stability than standing on foam. We required participants to stand on this disk on either two legs or one leg.

In both experiments, each participant performed each task under three attentional focus conditions. Under external focus conditions, participants were instructed to focus on rectangles that we had placed on the platform or the foam, and to put an equal amount of pressure on each rectangle. Under internal focus conditions, they were asked to focus on their feet, and to try to put an equal amount of pressure on each foot (solid surface) or to move their feet as little as possible (foam, disk). Finally, under control conditions, participants were simply instructed to "stand still."

The results turned out as one would expect on the basis of the constrained action hypothesis. In Experiment 1, there were no differences between focus conditions when participants stood on the solid surface, and there was only a small advantage on the foam surface when they adopted an external focus relative to an internal focus. Figure 4.5 shows the magnitude of sway under each focus condition for solid and foam tasks. In the second experiment, in which participants performed the more difficult task of standing on the rubber disk, the external focus condition resulted in greater stability (i.e., less sway) than both the internal focus and control conditions, and there was no significant difference between internal focus and control conditions (see figure 4.6). This was independent of whether participants were standing on one or two legs. Apparently, both tasks were sufficiently challenging to yield the "typical" performance benefits of an external focus.

What this study shows is that the extent to which the adoption of an external focus enhances performance depends on the difficulty of the task. It makes sense to assume that when the task is relatively simple and the performer is satisfied with the ongoing motor control processes, he or she is not tempted to intervene. That is, when postural sway or errors are small, performers are less prone to try to consciously control their movements. Thus, instructions to adopt an external focus would not be expected to provide additional advantages. In contrast, when a motor task is challenging and performers' attention is directed to the control of their movements (internal focus) or are left to their own devices (control condition), they are presumably more tempted to consciously intervene in those control processes. In this case, instructions to adopt an external focus provide performance (and learning) benefits.

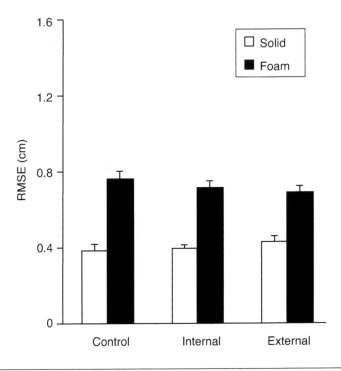

FIGURE 4.5 Magnitude of sway (root-mean-square error; RMSE) as a function of surface type (solid, foam) and type of attentional focus (control, internal, or external) in Experiment 1 of the study by Wulf, Töllner, and Shea (in press).

This might explain why some studies demonstrated no attentional focus effects or demonstrated them only under specific circumstances, namely when the task (or the test condition) was comparatively difficult. The implication for researchers is that the effects of attentional focus are best examined with tasks that are relatively challenging for the performer. For practitioners, these findings imply that giving external focus instructions or feedback is even more important when the task to be learned is difficult.

COMPLEXITY OF INSTRUCTIONS

In a few experiments, no performance differences were found between groups of novices who were given external versus internal focus instructions (Poolton et al., 2006; Castaneda & Gray, in press); or an external focus, even though it was more effective than

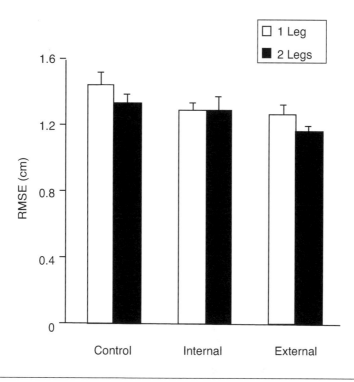

FIGURE 4.6 Magnitude of sway (root-mean-square error; RMSE) as a function of task (one-legged stance, two-legged stance) and type of attentional focus (control, internal, or external) in Experiment 2 of the study by Wulf, Töllner, and Shea (in press).

an internal focus, did not yield the typically found advantage compared to a control condition without focus instructions (Marchant, Clough, & Crawshaw, in press). In those cases, it appears that the complexity of the instructions may have thwarted any differential effects on learning. It is well known that beginners can easily be overwhelmed if they are given more than one or two instructions at a time (e.g., Schmidt & Wrisberg, 2004). Therefore, it might not be too surprising if giving them four or more sets of focus instructions at the same time, rather than one, cancels out any benefits external focus instructions might have.

For example, in the second experiment of their golf putting study, Poolton and colleagues (2006) gave their novice participants six sets of instructions under each of the internal or external focus conditions:

(1) Move your hands/the club back a short distance; (2) swing your hands/the club forward with a smooth action along a straight line; (3) allow your hands/the club to continue swinging a short distance after contact with the ball; (4) adjust the speed of your hands/the club so that the correct amount of force is applied; (5) adjust the angle of your hands/the club to attain the correct direction; and (6) keep your head still/focus on the ground for a few seconds after hitting the ball. These instructions were given before the beginning of practice; and after each block of 30 trials (with 10 blocks of trials), participants were reminded of the instructions and the importance of following them. The results showed no group differences during the practice phase or on the retention and transfer tests conducted afterward.

Aside from the fact that golf putting may not be a challenging enough task to be amenable to effects of attentional focus (as noted earlier), the amount of information participants had to process is likely a reason for the lack of an attentional focus effect in this study. Even though no control group was included, it is possible that participants' learning was degraded under both focus conditions to the extent that any potential benefits of the external focus instructions were nullified.

Similarly, in the dart throwing study by Marchant and colleagues (in press) that was described in chapter 2, four sets of instructions were given under internal or external focus conditions. Even though the external focus group showed greater throwing accuracy than the internal focus group, the external group was no more effective than the control group that was not given focus instructions. While one reason for this lack of advantage might be that the task itself promoted enough of an external focus (i.e., the target), another reason is presumably the complexity of the instructions in this study. As Marchant and colleagues point out themselves, "One explanation may be that the instructions used to manipulate an external focus in the present study were more complicated than those used in previous studies by Wulf and colleagues, which generally use a single cue. . . . With reduced complexity of the external instructions given, further benefits may have been demonstrated."

It is not only the complexity of the instructions per se that can apparently negate any advantages of an external focus, but also the complexity of the task and the situation in which performance takes place. An example is a study by Castaneda and Gray (in press) that used a simulated baseball batting task. Novices and experts performed under both internal and external focus conditions, with their attention directed to their hand movements or the movement of the bat, respectively. However, in contrast to what occurred in most previous attentional focus studies, participants were not simply instructed to direct their attention to these aspects of the task. Rather, they were presented with a computer-generated tone while they were batting and had to indicate afterward whether their hand or the bat was moving up or down at the time they heard the tone. (This was done in order to determine the extent to which participants actually directed their attention according to the instructions.) Thus, participants had to perform a secondary (judgment) task while they were engaged in the primary batting task. This is clearly more demanding than simply focusing on a certain part of the skill. It might therefore not be too surprising that there were no performance differences between internal and external focus conditions in novices. Experts, on the other hand, did show more effective batting performance when they were instructed to focus on the bat (external focus) compared to their hands (internal focus). This makes sense, though, because, as we discussed in chapter 1, experienced performers have more spare attentional capacity than novices and are less likely to be overwhelmed by the demands of a dual-task situation. The authors also acknowledged that the difference in the instructional methods between their study and previous studies could have been responsible for the lack of attentional focus effect in novice performers.

Overall, these findings suggest that external focus instructions are best limited to one cue at a time. This is especially true for novices, who might otherwise be easily overwhelmed by the amount of information, so that any advantages the external focus might have induced could be negated. You might recall that in several of our own studies, we also gave a number of different focus instructions (Wulf, Eder, & Parma, 2005) or feedback statements (Wulf et al., 2002). Yet in these cases, the instructions were spaced out, and the feedback statements were given one at a time. Thus, this might be an alternative approach, particularly when complex movement patterns have to be learned.

SUMMARY

Taken together, the findings we have discussed in this chapter provide converging evidence for the view that focusing on the movement effect, rather than on the movements themselves, is more effective *and* efficient. Not only does an external focus result in more effective movement outcomes, such as improved balance, greater accuracy in hitting a target, or faster movements; but the greater frequency of movement adjustments, the reduced attentional demands, and the reduced neuromuscular activity suggest that movement production is more efficient. These findings demonstrate how effectively our motor system functions if it is unhampered by conscious control attempts.

PRACTICAL APPLICATIONS

ATTENTIONAL CAPACITY

An external focus appears to reduce attentional demands, compared to an internal focus, thereby leaving more attentional capacity available for other aspects of the task. This means that more attention can be directed to the style or expression, which is an important component of some sport skills (e.g., in gymnastics or figure skating), or the strategy (e.g., in basketball, soccer, tennis, windsurfing). In situations that are inherently dangerous, such as motorcycle riding or car racing, the additional attentional capacity could be directed at potential hazards, such as other vehicles or the road conditions, or the optimal course.

- In what other situations might the availability of spare attentional capacity be advantageous?
- Think about how patients in physical or occupational therapy might benefit from greater spare attentional capacity.

HIGH-FREQUENCY ADJUSTMENTS

A high frequency of movement adjustments is important for all balance skills, as slow responses to perturbations increase the risk of falling and therefore pose a threat to an individual's postural stability. The high-frequency adjustments seen when people adopt an external focus should therefore be beneficial for skills requiring balance, such as ice-skating, riding a unicycle, skiing, walking on a tightrope, or surfing. In those cases, focusing on the implement or another (anticipated) movement effect, such as the intended path or line of progression, should enhance balance compared to focusing on actually "remaining in balance." Also, whenever possible, focusing on a more distant effect may be more beneficial than focusing on a close effect, as this seems to increase the frequency of responding even more.

- How would the distance effect apply to walking on a balance beam, for example?
- For which other skills might the speed in making adjustments or error corrections play a role?

NOISE REDUCTION

The greater efficiency in movement production seen under external relative to internal focus conditions has implications for a variety of motor skills. For instance, the reduction in "noise" due to unnecessary muscular activity appears to be one reason the outcome is more reliable in skills requiring accuracy. Skills like throwing or shooting an object at a target (e.g., in basketball, dart throwing, pistol shooting) or passing a ball to a teammate (e.g., in football, soccer, baseball) therefore benefit from an external focus.

- For which skills other than those requiring accuracy could "noise" reduction be relevant?
- How could one measure "noise" at a behavioral level?

ENERGY DEMANDS

An efficient movement technique, in which appropriate forces are produced in the appropriate direction and at the right time, is essential for many skills. Because it reduces energy demands, a good technique enables performers to maintain a given level of performance for a longer period of time (e.g., swim or run longer) or increase the performance level for a given amount of time (e.g., increase the distance in a 6 min run).

- Discuss how one could examine more directly how different attentional foci affect energy demands associated with the execution of a skill.
- In what ways might a weightlifter benefit from these effects?

FUTURE DIRECTIONS

BRAIN IMAGING

From a more theoretical perspective, it would be interesting to use brain imaging techniques, such as functional magnetic resonance imaging (fMRI), to further examine the hypothesis that an external focus results in greater automaticity in movement control than an internal focus (constrained action hypothesis). More direct evidence for this view would be provided if brain areas that control automated movements were more active when the individual adopted an external as compared to an internal focus while performing a motor task.

Is the most effective focus for hitting the ball the same for novice and expert players?

CHAPTER 5

LEVEL OF EXPERTISE

Movements often have more than one effect. For example, when players hit a golf ball, their movements have an effect not only on the motion of the club, but also on the trajectory and landing point of the ball. Which movement effect should one focus on? Is there an "optimal" attentional focus? If so, does this perhaps depend on the individual's experience with the task, that is, his or her level of expertise? Many expert golfers will tell you that they focus on where they want to ball to go. Perhaps this is most effective focus for them. Is this also the optimal focus for beginning golfers? Or is it be more effective for beginners to focus on something that is more related to movement technique, such as the movement of the golf club?

In the previous chapters, we have seen many examples of how directing attention to the effect, or anticipated outcome, of a movement can considerably speed up the learning process and enhance performance compared to directing attention to the movements themselves. While reading those chapters, you might have wondered which effect a performer should focus on if the movement has more than one effect. An interesting question is also whether the most effective focus might depend on the stage of learning and might change with the level of expertise.

Not many studies have addressed the question whether the optimal attentional focus varies with the level of expertise. Some studies, however, relate to this issue, and the results indicate that attentional focus effects may indeed depend on the amount of experience an individual has had with a certain task. In addition, the findings suggest that a task needs to be challenging enough for the performer—which, of course, also depends on his or her level of experience—in order for attentional focus effects to manifest themselves. In the following sections, we will take a look at those studies. We will see what they suggest about the optimal focus for beginners versus expert performers. The findings, in combination with theoretical conceptualizations of how we control our actions (e.g., Vallacher, 1993; Vallacher & Wegner, 1987), will at least give us some preliminary ideas about how performance (and learning) may be optimized through attention focusing at different stages of learning.

INSTRUCTION AND FEEDBACK IN NOVICE MOTOR LEARNING AND PERFORMANCE

In one of the first studies in which we examined whether different movement effects that a person can focus on might differ in their effectiveness, we had participants without golf experience hit golf balls to a target (Wulf et al., 2000, Experiment 2). This study was similar to the golf study we talked about in chapter 2 (Wulf, Lauterbach, & Toole, 1999), except that we compared two external focus groups (and did not have an internal focus group). One group of participants was instructed to focus on the club motion, whereas the other group was to focus on the anticipated trajectory of the ball and the target. Even though there were no group differences during the practice phase, the "club" group outperformed the "target" group in a retention test. That is, the club group showed significantly greater accuracy in their shots than the target group. Another study (Perkins-Ceccato, Passmore, & Lee, 2003) also showed that novice golfers don't do well when they are instructed to simply focus on the target compared to when they are given information that is more related to the technique. What is the reason for this? Why is it not very effective for beginners to simply focus on the target?

The problem that beginners face when they focus on "remote" effects, such as the trajectory of a golf ball, is that the movement effect cannot be directly related to the body movements that produced it. That is, there is no direct relationship between a given trajectory and a particular movement pattern, as the same trajectory could have been produced by different coordination patterns. This ambiguity makes the learning of the correct technique and the development of a stable movement pattern—which, after all, is the goal of learning—relatively difficult. This problem is reduced when a beginner directs attention to a less remote effect such as the movement of the golf club. Because the club motion is more directly related to the body movements, in both space and time, this effect can be associated more easily with the motor commands that caused the club motion. Clearly, for a beginner to learn an effective technique, it is necessary that she or he be able to associate the motor commands and the resulting movement effects.

In general, most studies of attentional focus effects have used relatively complex skills. Also, most studies used novice performers who had little or no experience with the respective task (for exceptions, see the golf study by Wulf [Experiment 2, in press] and the volleyball and soccer studies by Wulf et al. [2002]). Thus, the relative level of difficulty was comparatively high, making the task relatively challenging. In the last chapter, we discussed some exceptions: If the task is relatively simple and already affords an automatic mode of control, instructions inducing an external focus may not provide an additional benefit. As task difficulty is a function of the complexity of the task and the performer's experience with the task, a low level of difficulty would occur not only if the task was relatively simple (as discussed in chapter 4), but also if the task was relatively difficult and the performer had task-related experience. In either case, the motor skill would likely be controlled more or less automatically already. An interesting question is, Would we still see benefits of inducing an external focus if the performer is already an "expert"? Is it possible that external focus instructions can even be detrimental?

INSTRUCTION AND FEEDBACK IN EXPERT MOTOR LEARNING AND PERFORMANCE

ATTENTIONAL INSIGHTS

Adina Mornell is a renowned concert pianist and professor of instrumental pedagogy at the University of Music and the Dramatic Arts in Graz, Austria. Here she shares some interesting insights into the various facets of expertise of concert pianists, as well as the role their attentional focus plays in delivering a "perfect" performance.

Concert pianists are judged by their ability to give creative and inspired musical performances. The audience expects these professionals to play the correct notes. It is taken for granted that these artists will play flawlessly. Not a thought is given to the fact that this involves executing highly skilled motor tasks with utmost perfection.

In many ways, this is also what performers think–and should think. In order to deliver their utmost, they must remain focused on the musical message, on the emotional qualities of the work, on the overall structure of the composition, and *not* on the notes. The work that these experts have put in, innumerable hours of training over a period of years, even decades, enables them to concentrate on sound quality and expression, forgetting about technique and difficulty. Instead of delivering a routine performance fixed by repetitive practice, musicians are able to react flexibly to the environment. They are able to modify tone, tempo, and use of pedal, for example, to adapt to the acoustics of the hall. They can follow a spontaneous urge, deciding onstage to play a phrase with more flamboyance or introspection. This is achieved by listening to their fantasy. Once the goal is set and the sound imagined, they act. A high-level command is issued, eliciting a set of complex movements. There is no time for thought to be given to the 'what' or 'how' of creating this desired effect. This is musical expertise.

The mind-set of professionals involves not questioning actions, but rather having trust in their own abilities. No surprise then, that descriptions of optimal performance often include reference to 'flow' (e.g., Csikszentmihalyi, 1990), or to being in the 'zone.' Not to be confused with effortlessness, this state involves seamless coordination of intention and execution, in which human ability matches task difficulty and challenge. From an individual fingertip caressing a key to the entire body movement necessary to creating full sound upon impact–playing the piano means activating mind, body, and soul. The countless individual actions involved in each and every phrase are simply not readily available to cognition. Without automation of motor programs, this would not be possible. That is why experts learn to 'let go' in order to achieve, and why the desire to control can be so dangerous.

In performance, musicians' most valuable assets can become their worst enemies. The same finely tuned ear that enables musicians to weave intricate musical lines can suddenly pick up a disturbing sound in the hall. The same emotional sensitivity that generates beauty in their playing exposes musicians to vulnerability and self-doubt. In the moment concentration becomes interrupted, for whatever reason, self-consciousness is created. A sudden shift in attentional focus–towards what Gabriele Wulf defines as 'internal focus'–throws the brain engine into a lower gear with a loud roar and pulls the hand brake, disrupting a fluid glide through the musical composition. In short, nothing is worse for a musician than the sudden urge to deliberately manage movement, a departure from external focus. As logical and obvious as this sounds, there has been almost no empirical research done to date on this phenomenon.

Not very many studies have dealt with the effectiveness of internal versus external foci of attention in "expert" performers. In our study with novice and advanced volleyball players, we found that the two groups of performers benefited equally from feedback inducing an external focus rather than an internal focus in learning a volleyball serve (Wulf et al., 2002, Experiment 1). Similarly, individuals with experience in soccer showed improved learning (lofted soccer pass) when provided with feedback that induced an external relative to an internal focus (Wulf et al., 2002, Experiment 2). Finally, in one of our golf studies (Wulf, in press, Experiment 2), we had expert golfers, with handicaps of around 0, perform pitch shots. Similar to what we had done in the first experiment in that study (Wulf, in press, Experiment 1; see chapter 2), we asked the golfers to focus either on the swing of the club (external focus), on the swing of their arms (internal focus), or on what they normally focused on (control condition). All expert participants performed 20 shots under each condition. The results showed that the experts were more accurate when they adopted an external focus compared to the two other conditions, which resulted in similar accuracy scores (see figure 5.1). This is interesting because it shows that performance can be improved through external focus instructions not only at the beginning stages of learning, but even at a high level of expertise.

Even though the participants in our studies had considerable experience with the respective skills, they were not top-level performers. So, even for them there was still clearly room for improvement. In order to look at expert performance, one doesn't necessarily need world-class athletes. Every one of us can be considered an expert in some regard. Consider the skill of walking or simply standing still. Most of us are certainly experts at standing still on a solid surface (as opposed to children, who are just learning to stand upright, for example, or individuals whose motor system is compromised by disease or aging). Would instructing a young, healthy adult to focus on the pressure she or he is exerting on the surface (external

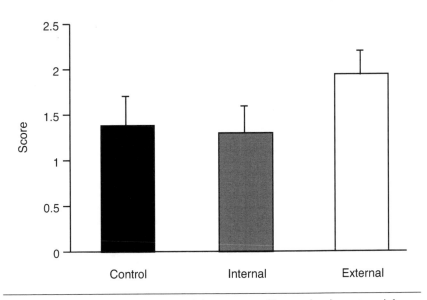

FIGURE 5.1 Accuracy scores of the expert golfers under the external focus, internal focus, and control conditions in the study by Wulf (in press, Experiment 2).

Adapted from Wulf and Su 2005.

focus), as compared to focusing on the pressure exerted by the feet (internal focus) or not focusing at all (control condition), result in greater stability? As we saw in chapter 4, the findings of one of our studies suggest that it does not. When people were standing on an even, noncompliant surface, the type of focus did not make a difference (Wulf, Töllner, & Shea, in press, Experiment 1). Even when participants stood on a foam surface (which might be a novel task, but is still relatively simple), there was no difference in the amount of sway. However, for more challenging balance tasks, the typical external focus advantages emerged. When participants were asked to stand on an inflated rubber disk (see figure 4.6), on either two legs or one leg, an external focus was more effective than an internal or no focus (Wulf, Töllner, & Shea, in press, Experiment 2). Thus, these findings provide preliminary support for the notion that attentional focus effects increase with an increase in task difficulty. If the task is already automated, there is nothing to be gained from inducing, or adopting, an external focus. The focus is presumably on standing still, and the motor system does what it has to do to achieve this effect.

But is this really comparable to situations in which highly skilled athletes perform a very difficult and complex motor skill? An interesting question is how performance at the highest skill level—such as that demonstrated by world-class athletes—would be affected by different types of attentional focus. While one would expect an internal focus to have detrimental effects on their performance (see chapter 1), even directing their attention to a direct, or proximal, movement effect (McNevin, Shea, & Wulf, 2003; Wulf et al., 2000) might be not only relatively ineffective, but perhaps even detrimental to their performance. If performance is already at or near the optimum level and controlled with a high degree of automaticity, directing performers' attention to an aspect of the task that they normally do not attend to might, in fact, negatively affect their performance (Vallacher, 1993; Vallacher & Wegner, 1987).

A recent study was the first to use highly skilled performers and a balance task that could be expected to be relatively easy for them (Wulf, 2006). We had the unique opportunity to test acrobats in the Cirque du Soleil show *Mystère* in Las Vegas, Nevada. All of them regularly performed balance stunts in the show, such as walking on balls or landing on top of a three-person pyramid after several somersaults (see photos). These athletes' balance capabilities can be assumed to be at or near the highest possible level. The task used in our study required them to stand still on an inflated rubber disk (see chapter 4). Thus, it was similar to, but clearly less difficult than, the stunts performed by most of them onstage. We gave the acrobats either no attentional focus instructions (control condition) or instructed them to focus on reducing movements of either their feet (internal focus) or the disk (external focus). All 10 individuals performed under all conditions.

Again, what we wanted to know was whether the benefits of an external focus would generalize to such a high level of task-related experience and skill. We suspected that, because the acrobats' performance was already optimal, inducing any type of focus that was different from what these performers typically focus on, if anything, might actually be detrimental. To see how the effects of different attentional focus conditions on the experts' performance compared to the effects on the performance of "normal" individuals, we included kinesiology students without special balance skills as a control group.

The results were interesting in several ways. First, acrobats (experts) had clearly less postural sway than the students (nonexperts) (see figure 5.2a). In fact, their sway was about 50% smaller than that of nonexperts. Second, the frequency of the movement adjustments in experts was generally higher relative to that in nonexperts (see figure 5.2b), reflecting a greater degree of automaticity in the control of posture (see chapter 4). Thus, expert balancers were able to compensate for deviations of their center of pressure very rapidly and effectively by using reflex-type control mechanisms. The result was greatly reduced sway and enhanced stability.

Performers in the Cirque du Soleil show *Mystère* in Las Vegas.

Photos: Al Seib. Costumes: Dominique Lemieux. © 1999, 2003 Cirque de Soleil Inc.

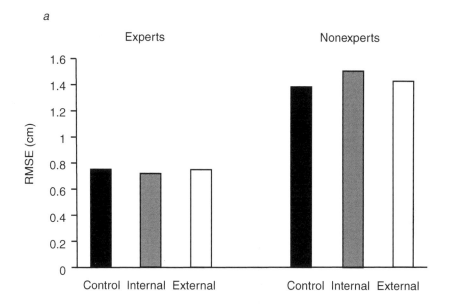

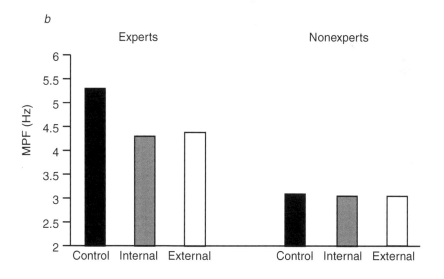

FIGURE 5.2 *(a)* Magnitude of sway (root-mean-square error) and *(b)* frequency of responding (mean power frequency) for experts and nonexperts as a function of the type of attentional focus (control, internal, or external).

Adapted from Wulf 2006.

Interestingly, even though the type of attentional focus did not differentially affect their postural sway, the experts had clearly higher mean power frequency values in the control condition compared to the conditions in which they directed their attention to the movements of the disk (external focus) or their feet (internal focus). Thus, the degree of automaticity—and stability—was greatest when experts were free to concentrate on whatever they focus on under normal conditions. Clearly, asking them to focus on movements of the disk (or their feet) was not beneficial for them; rather, it apparently resulted in a more conscious mode of control and hampered their stability.

For the nonexperts in this study, we did not find any differences between attentional focus conditions (although in a similar study we did find external focus benefits when healthy, young individuals were required to stand on one or two legs on the disk; Wulf, Töllner, & Shea, in press, Experiment 2). Apparently, the task was not challenging enough for these participants. As mentioned earlier, a certain degree of task difficulty seems to be required for attentional focus effects to manifest themselves. If automatic control strategies already exist due to prior experience, giving external focus instructions does not provide an additional advantage.

If it is true that attentional focus effects occur only if the task is challenging enough for the performer, then we should see benefits of an external focus in individuals for whom the task (i.e., standing on the disk) is more difficult. As mentioned earlier, people with Parkinson's disease (PD) are a population for whom balance problems are typical. Therefore, we did a follow-up study with older individuals (mean age: 71.1 years) with PD, using the same task and the same attentional focus conditions. Figure 5.3 depicts the amount of postural sway participants showed when they were instructed to focus on the movements of the disk (external focus) or on their feet (internal focus), and when they were not given focus instructions (control). As you can see, participants exhibited the least amount of sway when they focused externally. (There were no differences between focus conditions in the frequency of movement adjustments.) Thus, the population for which this task was quite challenging demonstrated the "typical" attentional focus effect, with an external focus resulting in significantly more effective performance than either internal focus or control conditions and with no difference between the latter two. This supports the view that the relative level of task difficulty (i.e., the difficulty of the task in relation to the performer's skill level) seems to be critical for external focus advantages to occur.

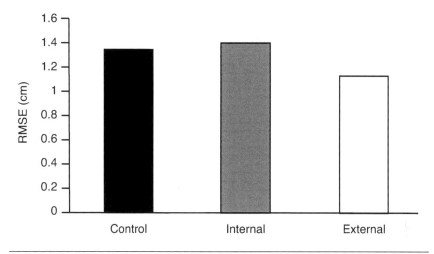

FIGURE 5.3 Magnitude of sway (root-mean-square error) for participants with Parkinson's disease as a function of the type of attentional focus (control, internal, or external) in the study by Wulf, Landers, & Töllner (2006).

Adapted from Wulf, Landers, and Töllner 2006.

Overall, it is clear that the type of attentional focus has a differential influence on performance for participants with different skills levels. For the group with balance impairments (participants with PD), postural stability was enhanced through external focus instructions; no attentional focus effects were found for the group of young adults (nonexperts); and postural stability was actually degraded through both internal and external focus instructions in expert balancers. In the following section we consider why the type of focus might interact with the level of expertise.

ACTION CONTROL AND ATTENTIONAL FOCUS

As individuals gain experience with a certain skill, and the movement becomes more and more automated, the action is assumed to be monitored at progressively higher levels. As Vallacher (1993) puts it, "[C]ontrol over the act moves towards higher levels of representation as the lower level features of the action become coordinated and thus capable of discharge without conscious monitoring" (p. 455). Such a hierarchy of goals might be to "win a tennis match," "hit an ace," "give the ball a topspin," and "flip the wrist." For example, hitting an ace would be a relatively high-level goal, while the steps required to achieve this goal would be represented at a lower level of the hierarchy, with muscle control being at the lowest level. Under certain conditions, such as social pressure to do well (e.g., engendered by the promise of a reward, the threat of punishment, or competition), however, individuals tend to focus on lower-than-optimal hierarchical levels of action control (e.g., Vallacher, 1993; Vallacher & Wegner, 1987). This would also be the case when performers are instructed to pay attention to the details of their actions. The result is that movements that are typically performed effectively and efficiently are disrupted. That is, attempts to consciously control an action that is normally controlled automatically essentially disintegrate it and take away its fluidity, sometimes resulting in "choking" (see chapter 1). Vallacher (1993) suggests that effective performance involves "knowing when to let go of an action allowing the elements of the queue to run off without further conscious intervention," and further that "consciousness can be overdone, functioning to subvert . . . effective action" (p. 461). For the acrobats, "standing still" on a compliant surface was presumably represented at the highest level of control, and basically all movements required to achieve this goal were controlled automatically. Asking them to focus on moving the disk (external focus) or their feet (internal focus) as little as possible directed their attention to a lower level of control and disrupted the fine-tuned, reflexive control mechanisms that normally govern their balance.

Even though the students were clearly less proficient than the experts, they appeared to have the basic balance skills that enabled them to stand on the disk without too much effort. Thus, instructions to adopt an external focus did not provide any additional advantages. In contrast, for the older participants with PD, the task was very challenging. Because participants perceived the instability and perhaps even experienced a certain degree of fear of losing their balance (despite the walker and the spotter who was providing support in this case), they presumably used more conscious control strategies—particularly under internal focus and control conditions. The result was a relatively large degree of sway. However, with an external focus, postural sway was significantly decreased. This suggests that participants utilized the automatic control processes they had available, which effectively enhanced their stability. It also suggests that they normally don't make use of these automatic control strategies, at least when dealing with novel or challenging situations.

The important point is that these participants, for whom the task was comparatively difficult, spontaneously chose a level of control that was lower than necessary, and thus nonoptimal. The external focus instructions promoted the use of higher-level control processes and led to more effective performance.

Thus, it seems clear that for different levels of expertise, different types of attentional foci are optimal. An interesting question is, therefore, what type of focus is optimal for a given level of expertise, as well as how the optimal focus changes across practice. This is discussed next.

OPTIMAL ATTENTIONAL FOCUS

As mentioned earlier, actions can be monitored at various hierarchical levels. Furthermore, as the skill level increases, individuals tend to control the action at higher levels. Along the same lines, a performer can focus on movement effects at different hierarchical levels, and that focus also changes with practice or experience. For example, while a novice typist might focus on the pressing the correct keys, a skilled typist, who has already developed motor programs for certain sequences of letters or words, might focus on whole words or even combinations of words. (A motor program is a prestructured set of commands that is sent to the muscles and is the basis for the automatic control of movements; Schmidt & Lee, 2005.) Similarly, a novice juggler might have to concentrate on throwing the balls in the right direction and with the appropriate amount of force, whereas an expert juggler might focus on the "cascading" pattern of ball trajectories. That is, while beginners typically focus on lower-level effects that are a direct consequence of their limb movements, or even on the control of their body movements themselves (internal focus), skilled performers tend to focus on higher-level effects of their actions. The balance acrobats presumably focused on a high-level consequence of the body movements, such as simply "standing still." Because of their extensive experience with this type of skill (e.g., standing on balls), this type of focus triggered the muscular activities necessary to achieve the effect. In contrast, directing their attention to a lower-level effect (e.g., the movements of the disk) disrupted the automatic control processes that they normally utilize.

In general, it seems reasonable to suggest that actions should always be controlled at the highest possible level. This way the performer takes advantage of available motor programs that control the action automatically. In fact, focusing on a higher-level effect may act to combine a series of motor programs into a larger unit, such that the whole action runs more smoothly and without interruption. For example, through a focus on the pattern of ball trajectories in juggling, the height and direction of the balls might be controlled more automatically (and more effectively) as a by-product. Of course, for novices who have not yet developed the necessary motor programs, it may not be feasible to focus on high-level effects. As mentioned earlier, for beginning golfers, focusing on a lower-level effect (e.g., motion of the golf club) is more effective than focusing on a higher-level effect (e.g., trajectory of the golf ball). Because this effect is more directly related to the movements that produced it, a focus on the club should facilitate the learning of the appropriate motor program. Thus, the optimal attentional focus depends on the level of expertise. In general, the focus should be on a movement effect that corresponds to the highest level of control that is feasible. Where exactly this level is, of course, depends on the relative difficulty of the task at hand and the task-related experience of the performer.

One might expect that individuals would spontaneously adopt the optimal focus of attention. Interestingly, however, this does not seem to be the case. In fact, when people are not given attentional focus instructions and are left to their own devices (control condition), their performance is typically similar to that seen under internal focus conditions, and less effective than under external focus conditions (Landers et al., 2005; McNevin & Wulf, 2002; Wulf, Höß, & Prinz, 1998, Experiment 1; Wulf & McNevin, 2003; Wulf et al., 2003). This indicates that individuals tend to choose a lower than necessary level of control. The reason might be that people are inclined to be relatively cautious when confronted with novel and complex motor tasks, especially those involving balance. The problem is that this does not result in optimal performance; ironically, it typically degrades performance. Of course, the good news is that performance can be improved almost immediately by a simple shift in the attentional strategy.

SUMMARY

A precondition for attentional focus effects to occur seems to be that the task poses at least somewhat of a challenge for the performer. If the task is very simple, no external focus advantages should be expected, as the action is already controlled automatically. If the task is relatively complex and challenging, performance advantages resulting from an external compared to an internal focus are seen across a wide range of levels of expertise. However, even though studies directly addressing this issue are lacking, it seems plausible to assume that the optimal focus changes with the level of expertise. While for beginners it might be most effective to focus on a "low-level" effect (e.g., one that can be directly related to the movements that produced it), experts might benefit more from focusing on a "high-level" effect (e.g., the overall outcome of the action) that could trigger all the submovements necessary to achieve this effect. Performers should focus on a movement effect that corresponds to the highest level of control that is feasible (given the difficulty of the task and the performer's experience with the task).

PRACTICAL APPLICATIONS

OPTIMAL EXTERNAL FOCUS

If the optimal (external) focus indeed changes with the performer's level of experience, such that lower-level, or more direct, effects are more effective early in the learning process and higher-level effects are more effective later, this would have implications for the performance of skills that have several distinguishable effects. For example, in sports in which implements (e.g., racket, club, bat, hockey stick) are used to strike an object (e.g., ball, puck), it might be advantageous in the early learning stages to direct learners' attention to the movement of the implement. This way, the proper technique is more likely to be acquired than if they are instructed to focus on the resulting trajectory of the ball, for instance. However, once the movement pattern has become relatively automated, focusing on the intended ball trajectory might be more beneficial than focusing on the movement of the implement. Eventually, at a high level of expertise, focusing on the goal (e.g., target, intended location of the ball) might be the most effective.

- What might a music teacher direct a flutist's attention to as the flutist becomes more proficient?
- Would you expect the (optimal) attentional focus of a racecar driver to change over the years of racing?

HIERARCHY OF MOVEMENT EFFECTS

Provided that the optimal focus varies as a function of the performer's expertise, there are two ways in which coaches, instructors, or performers themselves could make a mistake in deciding what attention should be directed to: The focus could be on a movement effect that is either too "low" or too "high" in the hierarchy of movement effects that one could potentially focus on. Is the risk of erring in one direction greater than that of erring in the other? It is difficult to give a general answer to this question, especially given the dearth of studies related to this issue. Yet, at least one finding suggests that a relatively low-level external focus might perhaps be less harmful than a focus that corresponds to too high a level of control: the finding that expert golfers (with handicap of 0) benefited from instructions to focus on the motion of the golf club (a low-level effect). When it comes to top-level performance, however, the danger of focusing on too "low" an effect increases. It is up to practitioners to experiment with different attentional foci, as well as to researchers to conduct studies that further our understanding of how the effectiveness of different attentional foci interacts with performers' level of expertise.

- What would be a hierarchy of movement effects that an experienced gymnast or springboard diver could focus on?
- What are the risks of focusing on effects that are too "low" or too "high," respectively?

FUTURE DIRECTIONS

CHOKING UNDER PRESSURE

Performance decrements in stressful situations are a common phenomenon (see chapter 1). There is good evidence that a major cause of choking is "self-focused" attention. Yet, what exactly is it that athletes or musicians, for example, focus on when they are under pressure to perform well? Do they focus too much on controlling their movements? That is, do they adopt an internal focus? If so, could practicing with an external focus prevent, or at least reduce, choking? Also, could the decision to adopt an external focus in the pressure situation itself result in an immediate improvement in performance?

EXPERTISE

Another fruitful direction for future research would be to examine how performers' level of expertise interacts with their focus of attention. Empirical investigations into whether the optimal focus indeed changes with the level of experience, as outlined in this chapter, could lead to findings that potentially have important implications. Such work might not only result in a better understanding of whether and how the learning process can be facilitated by changing the type of attentional focus throughout practice; it might also lead to more specific recommendations for how expert performance (e.g., in sports or music) could be enhanced through attentional focus training.

The postural system makes spontaneous adjustments to help us achieve our suprapostural goal. Yet the effectiveness of those adjustments depends on the type of attentional focus.

CHAPTER 6

SUPRAPOSTURAL TASKS

Watching circus acrobats is always fascinating. Some of these performers show amazing balancing stunts, such as standing on several layers of cylinders with different orientations in the horizontal plane, so that minor deviations of the center of mass in either direction could cause the whole "tower" (with the acrobat on top) to collapse. What is even more impressive is when the performer proceeds to juggle on this highly unstable support surface. The whole stunt becomes even more dangerous and thrilling, as one intuitively expects the second task (juggling) to take away some of the attentional resources that could be directed toward balancing—which should have a detrimental effect on balance performance. However, it appears that the opposite is actually the case: When the acrobat starts to juggle, he or she actually becomes *more* stable! That is, the sway is reduced. It appears that the additional task, rather than having a detrimental effect on balance, in fact enhances it. How can this phenomenon be explained?

This chapter extends the discussion of attentional focus effects on motor performance to a special type of task, namely tasks that involve *suprapostural* goals. These are skills in which our postural, or balance, system subserves a "higher" goal (e.g., juggling on an unstable surface). These skills are particularly interesting as the type of focus on the suprapostural task not only influences suprapostural performance, but also indirectly affects postural control. These findings have implications for training procedures used in rehabilitation settings.

An experimental demonstration of the enhancement of postural stability through the addition of a suprapostural task, as well as an explanation for this interesting phenomenon, has been provided by Michael Riley and colleagues (Riley et al., 1999). These authors measured postural sway when participants, standing upright with their eyes closed, touched a curtain very lightly with their fingertips. (A curtain, as opposed to a solid stationary object, was used because it did not provide any mechanical support for posture.) Participants were instructed to minimize any movements of the curtain resulting from their touch. The interesting finding was that touching the curtain significantly reduced postural fluctuations compared to not touching it. Riley and colleagues interpreted this result as indicating that the addition of a suprapostural goal (i.e., keeping the curtain still) resulted in spontaneous reductions in postural fluctuations to facilitate the achievement of the suprapostural goal. Thus, without our conscious involvement—and probably even without our awareness—the postural control system does what it has to do to help us achieve our (suprapostural) goals. This explains why the acrobat juggling on the tower of cylinders appears to be more stable as he or she starts to juggle. This is another amazing example of the automatic control capabilities of the motor system!

TYPE OF ATTENTIONAL FOCUS

Yet, one can ask an interesting question: Does it matter what the acrobat focuses on? Given that we are dealing with an experienced juggler (and balancer), it seems safe to assume that the acrobat focuses on the cascading patterns of the balls, for example, rather than being concerned with producing the right amount of force with each hand. But what would happen if the juggler started to focus on his or her arms? How would this affect juggling performance, and, even more interestingly, would it have an effect on postural stability? Or, more generally speaking, does the influence of suprapostural tasks on postural stability depend on whether one adopts an external or internal attentional focus on the suprapostural task?

From the study by Riley and colleagues (1999) it is not entirely clear whether participants' attention was directed more toward keeping their finger still (internal focus) in order to minimize movements of the curtain or more toward keeping the curtain still (external focus). If participants' attention was primarily directed to the movements of the curtain, that is, the *effects* of their (finger) movements, perhaps the reduction in postural sway was due to the external focus that these instructions induced. If this was indeed the case, would instructions that induced an internal focus, for example, by directing individuals' attention to their finger movements, have the same effect on postural control, or would the beneficial effect disappear?

This is an interesting question, because in our previous attentional focus research using balance tasks, performers were typically instructed to focus on the movements of their feet (internal focus) or on the effects of their movements on the support surface (external focus), but in either case attention was directed to the primary (i.e., balance) task. Thus, we wanted to examine whether instructions that induce an external versus internal focus with regard to a suprapostural task have an effect on the performance, and perhaps learning, of the postural task.

Therefore, Nancy McNevin and I (McNevin & Wulf, 2002) tried to replicate the study by Riley and colleagues (1999), but with an explicit attentional focus manipulation. Similarly to Riley and colleagues, we measured participants' postural sway while they were lightly touching a curtain with their fingertips. All participants were instructed to minimize movements of the curtain; but under one condition, participants were instructed to minimize curtain movements by focusing on the curtain itself (external focus), while under another condition they were instructed to minimize curtain movements by focusing on minimizing finger movements (internal focus). We also compared these two focus conditions to a control condition without the curtain (and without attentional focus instructions). Participants had their eyes closed under all conditions.

While we didn't find differences in the amount of postural sway, the type of attentional focus did influence the frequency of responding. Remember, a higher frequency of movement adjustments is thought to reflect a greater degree of automaticity in postural control, as more reflex-based control mechanisms (as opposed to conscious mechanisms) are used (see chapter 4). Indeed, external focus instructions promoted higher-frequency, lower-amplitude postural adjustments than did internal focus instructions or no instructions (control condition). That is, when participants focused on minimizing movements of the curtain, postural adjustments were small and very rapid. In contrast, when these same individuals attempted to minimize movements of the finger on the curtain, the frequency and amplitude of postural adjustments were no different than those recorded during quiet standing without touching the curtain (control condition). Thus, the different attentional focus instructions promoted different motor control strategies, which consequently led to differences in postural stability: Postural stability was enhanced when participants adopted an external focus. These findings are interesting, and they nicely extended our previous research because they showed that balance could be influenced not only directly through manipulation of the attentional focus on the balance task, but also *indirectly* through manipulation of the attentional focus on a suprapostural task.

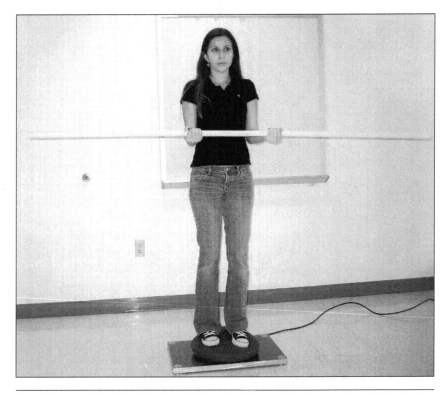

Participant balancing on a disk and holding a wand.

One question we haven't addressed yet is whether suprapostural task performance would also benefit from the adoption of an external focus. In the example just discussed, would your finger also be more stable if you focused on the curtain you were touching, rather than on your finger? While we did not measure movements of the curtain or the finger in that study, we did look at suprapostural task performance in another study (Wulf, Mercer, McNevin, & Guadagnoli, 2004). There the balance task was more challenging because participants had to stand on an inflated rubber disk (see photo). In addition, they were asked to hold a 2 m (2.2 yd) wand horizontal. We measured the stability of the wand, as well as the amount of postural sway.

The results replicated those of the previous study with regard to postural stability: When participants were instructed to focus on the wand (external focus), they had less postural sway than when they were instructed to focus on their hands (internal focus). In addition, the results showed that the wand was more stable when they adopted an external as opposed to an internal focus. Thus, the external focus on the suprapostural task had a double advantage. It enhanced performance on the suprapostural task, *and* it improved postural stability.

While these things are interesting to know, you might wonder whether these findings have any implications for your daily life (that is, even if you are not a circus acrobat). There certainly are a number of situations for which these results clearly seem to have implications. For instance, say you are painting the bathroom walls blue, and you are trying to avoid getting blue paint on the white ceiling. In some cases, this requires that you stand on the very top of the ladder (where the sign says, "DANGER—Do not stand or sit!"). If you want to paint a straight line, *and* if you don't want to fall off the ladder, what should you focus on? The answer is clear: Don't focus on moving your hand evenly, but rather focus on the line that the paintbrush is producing.

Standing still, even on an unstable surface, is an activity that is typically well learned and highly automated. It is therefore astounding that our motor system is able to make adjustments to further optimize our performance, depending on what our goal is. Not only that, it does this automatically and without our awareness. As we have seen, however, what we focus our attention on can have a significant influence on how well we perform. Sometimes—especially if the task is easy, or if we have a lot of experience with it—we might

© Human Kinetics

Moving attentional focus to the line should not only increase your chances of actually ending up with a straight line, but should also enhance your balance on top of the ladder and reduce the risk of falling from the ladder. (Believe me, you want to avoid that—and a resulting ACL tear and seemingly never-ending rehabilitation process!—which, however, is conducive to writing a book.)

spontaneously adopt the optimal (external) focus (as discussed in chapter 5). In many other situations, though, consciously adopting an external focus can considerably improve our performance. Somewhat ironically, this conscious decision serves to "free up" our motor system and let its automatic control capabilities take over. So, do we always need to remind ourselves to adopt an external focus if we want to perform as well as we can? Fortunately, there is some evidence that this might not be necessary. Adopting an external focus while practicing a balance task not only has immediate effects on performance, but also actually has beneficial long-term effects on learning, even if the external focus is no longer maintained. Some of the evidence for this is reviewed next.

TYPE OF ATTENTIONAL FOCUS AND ENHANCED LEARNING OF BALANCE TASKS

One piece of evidence suggesting that practicing with an external focus has benefits for learning, in that these benefits remain present even when we are not able to adopt an external focus, is the Pedalo study that we discussed earlier (Totsika & Wulf, 2003). Here participants were "distracted" on one of the transfer tests by being required to count backward by threes. Individuals who had adopted an external focus during practice still performed better under these conditions than individuals who had adopted an internal focus during practice. In addition, the study demonstrated that the advantages of practicing with an external focus generalize to novel variations of the task, in this case riding the Pedalo backward, or under time pressure, or both. This is good news, as it suggests that practicing with an external focus has generalizable and long-lasting effects.

Here, however, we are more concerned with the attentional focus on suprapostural tasks and its effect on postural stability. Imagine that you are a waitress or a waiter on in-line skates. (At one restaurant in Las Vegas, waiters and waitresses actually do wear skates.) Would focusing on the tray, as compared to your hands, not only allow you to keep the tray more stable and spill fewer drinks, but also enhance your in-line skating skills? And, furthermore, would your skating skills benefit from the external focus on the suprapostural task (focus on the tray) relatively permanently—and even if you were not carrying a tray? While it might seem hard to believe, there is actually some evidence that balance skills can benefit from practicing with an external focus on a suprapostural task.

In one study, we had participants balance on the stabilometer, and we added a suprapostural task: Participants had to hold a wooden tube horizontal with a table tennis ball in it (Wulf et al., 2003) (see photo). Instead of manipulating the attentional focus related to the balance task itself (as we had done in previous studies), however, we gave internal or external focus instructions related to this task. While participants in the internal focus group were instructed to focus on keeping their hands horizontal, participants in the external focus group were instructed to focus on keeping the tube horizontal. We were particularly interested in how the *learning* of a novel balance (postural) task would be affected by the suprapostural task. To examine the relatively permanent, or learning, effects that attentional focus on the suprapostural task had on the postural (balance) task, we included a transfer test in which the suprapostural task was removed. This allowed us to assess the remaining effects, if any, of the attentional focus manipulation on balance learning. Therefore, after two days during which participants practiced the balance task concurrently with the suprapostural task, they performed a retention test with the suprapostural task (but without instructions or reminders regarding their attentional focus) and a transfer test without the suprapostural task.

The results of this study are interesting for various reasons. First, performance on the suprapostural task (holding the tube horizontal) was more effective if participants adopted an external focus compared to an internal focus. We counted the number of times the ball in the tube contacted either end of the tube. If one considers these errors, the number of errors, throughout practice and retention, was clearly higher for individuals who focused on keeping their

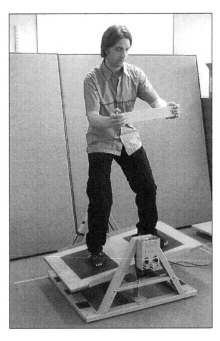

Participant balancing on the stabilometer while trying to hold a tube horizontal.

hands horizontal (internal focus) relative to those who focused on keeping the tube horizontal (external focus) (see figure 6.1). In fact, errors for the internal focus group were, on average, 130% larger during practice and 400% larger during retention than those for the external focus group. Interestingly, the external focus advantages were already seen early in practice. This is also in line with previous studies (e.g., Wulf, Lauterbach, & Toole, 1999; Wulf et al., 2002) and again shows the immediate and powerful effects of the attentional focus manipulation.

Second, and more importantly, the results showed that the attentional focus adopted on a suprapostural task influenced not only performance on the suprapostural task, but also performance on the postural task. The adoption of an external relative to an internal focus on the suprapostural task not only benefited performance on

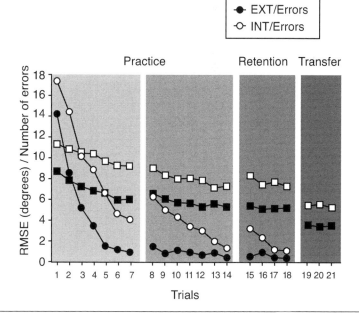

FIGURE 6.1 Deviations of the stabilometer platform from the horizontal (root-mean-square error) and errors on the suprapostural task for the external and internal focus groups in the study by Wulf and colleagues (2003, Experiment 1).

Reprinted, by permission, from G. Wulf et al., 2003, "Attentional focus on supra-postural tasks affects balance learning," *Quarterly Journal of Experimental Psychology* 56A: 1191-1211.

this task, but also enhanced balance performance. Again, the differential effects of the type of attentional focus on balance were seen early on in practice and remained present throughout the two days of practice, as well as during retention and transfer. It is particularly interesting that the beneficial effects of an external focus were also seen in *transfer*, that is, when participants performed the balance task without the suprapostural task. Thus, even though the two groups performed the balance task under exactly the same conditions in transfer (i.e., without the suprapostural task and the associated attentional foci), the attentional focus adopted during practice still influenced balance. That is, the suprapostural task effect was not only immediate, occurring while the suprapostural task was performed in concert with the balance task; rather, it had a relatively permanent effect on the *learning* of the balance task, as balance was still affected when the suprapostural task was removed.

One question you might ask is whether balancing on the stabilometer without a suprapostural task would not have resulted in better balance learning. After all, learners could have concentrated exclusively on the balance task instead of worrying about holding an object horizontal while balancing. Or, more specifically, would adopting an external focus on the suprapostural task produce more effective balance learning compared to balancing without a suprapostural task goal? Interestingly, the answer is yes. In a follow-up experiment, we compared groups who focused on keeping the hands (internal focus) or the tube (external focus) horizontal, as well as a control group (Wulf et al., 2003, Experiment 2). Control group participants were asked to hold the tube with both hands in front of their abdomen, but were not given any attentional focus instructions. The reason control participants were also required to hold the tube was that otherwise they would have been able to use their arms for balance control, which facilitates the maintenance of balance. Thus, in order to make the groups comparable, they all had to hold the tube. The important point, however, is that the control group participants did not have to worry about holding it horizontal, and could therefore concentrate fully on the stabilometer task.

The results of this experiment suggested that an external focus on the suprapostural task was, in fact, beneficial for balance learning. Even though the external focus group did not differ significantly from the control group in retention, the external focus group was superior to both the control and internal focus groups in transfer (see figure 6.2). It might not be too surprising that the external focus and

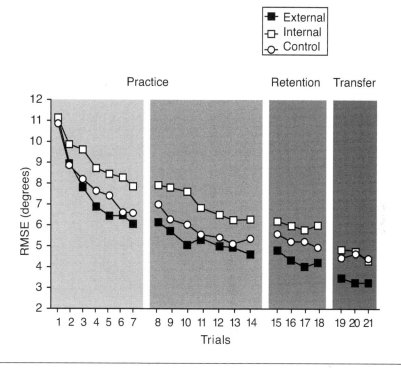

FIGURE 6.2 Deviations of the stabilometer platform from the horizontal (root-mean-square error) for the external focus, internal focus, and control groups in the study by Wulf and colleagues (2003, Experiment 2).

Reprinted, by permission, from G. Wulf et al., 2003, "Attentional focus on supra-postural tasks affects balance learning," *Quarterly Journal of Experimental Psychology* 56A: 1191-1211.

control groups did not differ in retention. The external (and internal) group participants might have remembered the attentional focus instructions given to them during practice and therefore maintained their focus on the suprapostural task. The control group participants, on the other hand, who were not given any focus instruction, could dedicate all of their attentional resources to the balance task. This might not only have led to the control group's relatively good performance during the practice phase, but presumably also have affected their performance during retention. However, when the suprapostural task was withdrawn in transfer, resulting in *identical* conditions for all groups, the learning advantages of the external focus condition, compared to both the internal and control conditions, were obvious.

So, what do these findings mean for you if you are a waiter or waitress cruising through the restaurant on skates? They suggest that if you focus on keeping the tray horizontal (rather than focusing on your hands), your in-line skating skills will improve automatically as well! This is obviously good news. Not only does the external focus directly benefit the (suprapostural) task that you focus on; it also has an indirect advantageous effect on postural performance, even if it involves the learning of a novel balance task. The results might have implications for other skills that have a suprapostural task goal as well. These might include figure skating (where the male partner lifts the female partner), shot put, discus throwing, or

If a rehabilitation patient's task is to take a pillow out of the top part of a linen closet, the physical therapist could direct her attention to the shape or weight of the pillow instead of her stance or arm extension.

windsurfing. In those and similar sports, an external focus on the object (or person) one is manipulating could have a positive influence on balance as well.

You might wonder whether adopting an external focus on a postural task (e.g., the movement of an unstable surface you are balancing on) would have beneficial effects on suprapostural task performance similar to those from an external focus on the suprapostural task itself. If the external focus on the balance task enhances postural control, perhaps this would, in turn, facilitate the achievement of the suprapostural task goal. Interestingly, the influence that the attentional focus on the suprapostural task has on postural task performance appears to be stronger than the reverse influence (Wulf, Mercer, McNevin, & Guadagnoli, 2004). While an external relative to an internal focus on the suprapostural task enhances postural task performance, an external focus on the postural task does not necessarily benefit suprapostural task performance. This makes sense, however, given that the act of balancing subserves the achievement of the suprapostural task goal. For example, if the goal is not to spill a bowl of soup while one walks across the dining room, success will depend on how stable one's gait pattern is. Thus, one would expect to see influences on postural performance as a function of the suprapostural task (e.g., Balasubramaniam & Turvey, 2000; Riley et al., 1999; Stoffregen et al., 2000).

It is possible that an external relative to an internal focus directed at the suprapostural task goal enhances postural stability because focusing on the outcome of the action tweaks the control mechanisms to achieve suprapostural *and* postural stability. In contrast, the type of focus on the postural task has a relatively minor effect on the performance of the suprapostural task. This can best be explained by the absence of a suprapostural task goal. Even though one might still be performing a suprapostural task, if attention is directed to the postural task, the suprapostural task becomes, at best, secondary. Therefore, it is perhaps not too surprising that the different attentional foci on the postural task do not have much of an effect on the suprapostural task. The fact that suprapostural task goals have a stronger influence on postural control than vice versa can be seen as reflecting the economy of the motor system: Control effort is invested only to the extent necessary for the accomplishment of the goal. That is, the motor system seems to optimize control processes based on the desired movement effect.

SUMMARY

As we have seen in this chapter, attentional focus effects generalize to tasks that have a suprapostural goal, such as holding an object still. That is, adopting an external focus on the suprapostural task (e.g., focusing on the object) enhances suprapostural task performance compared to adopting an internal focus (e.g., focusing on one's hands). Interestingly, this is achieved not only through enhanced upper limb control, but also through more effective postural control. Furthermore, an external focus on the suprapostural task facilitates performance not only while the individual adopts that focus (and performs a suprapostural task); even the learning of a balance, or postural, task can be enhanced as seen by balance performance when the suprapostural task is removed.

PRACTICAL APPLICATIONS

SUPRAPOSTURAL ACTIVITIES IN SPORT

The performance of skills that involve suprapostural activities may be enhanced if the individual adopts an external focus on the suprapostural task. For example, a discus thrower focusing on the trajectory of the discus in her hand may find that this improves not only the acceleration of the discus, but also her balance. Similarly, an external focus on the suprapostural task might benefit balance control in skills such as shot put, dart throwing, target shooting, or archery.

- Hammer throwing is a very complex activity requiring precise postural as well as suprapostural task control. Discuss how attentional focus instructions might influence the learning of different components of this skill.
- What other sport skills involve suprapostural tasks and might benefit from an external focus?

SUPRAPOSTURAL TASKS IN DAILY ACTIVITIES

Tasks involving suprapostural goals are part of many daily activities. Therefore, they are often practiced in rehabilitation settings. Therapists could take advantage of the external focus benefits found for suprapostural tasks by giving appropriate instructions. A therapist who has patients play "badminton" with a balloon could instruct them to focus on the balloon or the racket, rather than on their balance or arm movements (Barth,

2005). The external focus on the suprapostural task might have the double advantage of facilitating suprapostural and postural control.

- In the rehabilitation of knee or ankle injuries, physical therapists often make use of suprapostural tasks to improve patients' balance, by having them stand on a disk while throwing and catching balls, for example. What might be the rationale for the use of those tasks?
- What instruction should a therapist give to enhance balance training?

FUTURE DIRECTIONS

NATURE OF ADJUSTMENTS

The motor system has the remarkable capability of making postural adjustments in such a way that the achievement of suprapostural goals is facilitated. The exact nature of the adjustments depends on the constraints of the task, though. In some cases, suprapostural task goals are best accomplished if the joints are stiffened (e.g., if the objective is to keep an object still). In other cases, it is more advantageous to keep the joints flexible so that one can quickly respond to perturbations (e.g., when carrying a tray on a plane during turbulence). What are the underlying mechanisms for these adjustments? And how does the focus of attention modify the control processes to yield the differential effects on suprapostural and postural task performance that we have seen in this chapter? These are some of the issues that might be interesting to examine in future studies.

There is a need for developing physiotherapy interventions that can enhance balance in people with Parkinson's disease.

© Human Kinetics

CHAPTER 7

SPECIAL POPULATIONS

In the United States, between 1 and 1.5 million people suffer from Parkinson's disease. Parkinson's disease is a progressive neurodegenerative disease that is typically associated with a variety of motor problems, including tremor and deterioration of balance and postural control. A consequence of these problems is an increased likelihood of falling. Falls, in turn, can lead to severe injuries (e.g., head injuries, fractures) and to hospitalization, the need to use a wheelchair, or both. Interestingly, postural instability, which is presumably a causative factor of falls in persons with Parkinson's disease, appears to be resistant to dopaminergic therapy (Koller et al., 1989).

This chapter extends the discussion of attentional focus effects on motor performance to "special" populations. In particular, it concerns children, people who are elderly, and patient populations (e.g., persons with Parkinson's disease, cerebrovascular accident). As you will see, instructions to adopt an external focus enhance the performance of motor skills in these populations as well. Some of these findings have implications for training procedures used in rehabilitation settings. In addition, there is some preliminary evidence that attentional focus instructions also have an effect on oral-motor control, which may have implications for speech therapy.

CHILDREN

The evidence for external focus advantages we have looked at so far has been restricted, for the most part, to studies that used young and healthy adults, 20 to 30 years of age, as participants. What about younger people? Would children also benefit from instructions that direct their attention to the effects of their movements? Or are they less inclined to exert conscious control over their movements than adults typically are, and do they perhaps spontaneously focus more on the outcome of their actions?

Very few studies on attentional focus have used children as participants. (One reason might be that getting permission to conduct research with children is more difficult than using adult participants, as it includes getting informed consent from parents or guardians, as well as school administrators.) Jenifer Thorn at Florida State University in Tallahassee conducted a study with children, ages 9 to 12 years, to examine whether their balance performance would differ as a function of the focus instructions given to them (Thorn, 2006). Thorn used a Biodex Balance System (see photo), which consists of a movable force platform that measures a person's postural sway. The task can be made more or less difficult through adjustments in the stability level of the platform. There are eight stability levels, 1 being the least stable and 8 being the most stable level. On the basis of the results of a pilot study, Thorn chose level 3 for her participants. This level proved to be relatively challenging for children of that age group. The children were assigned to groups that were instructed either to "keep their feet still" (internal focus group) or to "keep the platform still" (external focus group). Each child performed several practice trials under one of these two conditions. Two days later,

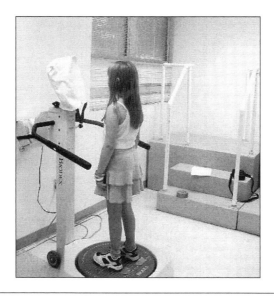

Participant using the Biodex Balance System. The monitor of the apparatus was covered so that participants wouldn't receive feedback about their stability, which might have directed their attention away from the attentional focus instructions given to them.

each child came back and completed a retention test, for which no attentional focus instructions were given.

Thorn also added an interesting feature to her experiment, namely a questionnaire, in which she asked the participants what they were "thinking about" when they were standing on the balance platform. While it is probably fairly safe to assume that adult participants typically follow the instructions given to them and use the attentional focus they are instructed to use (although there is no guarantee, of course), Thorn wanted to be sure that the children actually focused on their feet or the platform, respectively. (As we all know, kids are easily distracted.) It turned out that this was a good idea: Not all children did use the instructed attentional focus. However, among those who did, the children who were asked to keep the platform still showed less postural sway than those who were told to keep their feet still. That is, children who adopted the external focus demonstrated more effective balance performance after the two-day retention interval.

The fact that even children as young as 9 to 12 years can benefit from external focus instructions has important implications for physical education. Thorn's findings suggest that teachers should make an effort to word the instructions they give their students in such a way that their attention is directed to the movement outcome. Even if children are not always attentive and might not continuously maintain the instructed focus, external focus instructions should nevertheless have a more beneficial influence on learning than instructions that direct their attention to their own movements. The success experience resulting from this is especially important at a young age. Such success might not only increase students' motivation for continued practice, but even motivate them to take up other sports and to keep playing sports throughout adolescence and adulthood.

AGING

Older people often need to learn new motor skills, such as walking with a cane or a walker or using a wheelchair. Could the learning of motor skills be enhanced in older individuals as well, if they were given attentional focus instructions? Also, many daily-life activities become more challenging as we get older. Activities like climbing a ladder to clean the windows, riding a bicycle, or simply carrying a cup of coffee become more difficult. Do people spontaneously adopt the optimal attentional focus when performing these skills, or could their performance be improved if they were given external focus instructions? Sometimes motor problems are exacerbated by diseases, such as Parkinson's disease, or traumatic brain injury (stroke). Could therapeutic intervention be made more effective if physical or occupational therapists used instructions or feedback that induced an external rather than internal focus? Even though there are only a few studies on such questions so far, the results are encouraging.

Eye–hand coordination is required in many activities of daily living, such as chopping mushrooms, eating with a knife and fork, writing, or driving a car. As reaction time and the speed of responses typically decrease with age, we wanted to know whether instructing older individuals to adopt an external focus could enhance their performance on a task that required the coordination of visual information and hand movements. This might have practical implications for a variety of real-life tasks, including those that are potentially dangerous (e.g., cutting vegetables). In one study, we compared performances of older adults (average age, 70 years) to those of young adults (average age, 21 years) on a pursuit-rotor tracking task (Weir et al., 2005). Participants, standing in front of the apparatus, attempted to track a target light, which was moving vertically in a circle, with a stylus. The end of the stylus was bent in a 90° angle, and participants held the stylus vertically in a power grip such that the thumb extended horizontally toward the pursuit rotor. All participants performed several 25 s trials under each of two attentional focus conditions. For the internal focus condition, they were instructed to focus on "keeping the knuckle of (their) thumbs centered within the target"; for the external focus condition they were instructed to focus on "keeping the tip of the stylus centered within the target." All participants performed under two target speeds: one rotation per second (1 Hz) or one rotation per 2 s (0.5 Hz). As we saw in chapter 4, the difficulty of the task seems to influence the "size" of the attentional focus effects (e.g., Landers et al., 2005; Wulf, Töllner, & Shea, in press). Therefore, we expected to see greater external focus advantages on the more difficult (i.e., faster) tracking task.

The average time during which participants had the cursor on the target is shown in figure 7.1 for each age group, as well as for target speed and focus condition. Not surprisingly, younger adults

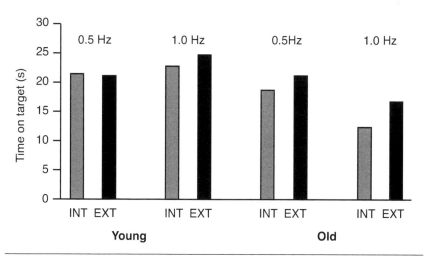

FIGURE 7.1 Time on target for young and older adults under each speed (0.5, 1.0 Hz) and attentional focus condition (internal, external).

generally performed more effectively than older adults. More interestingly, when participants focused on the stylus (external), their time on target was greater than when they focused on the knuckle of their thumb (internal), even though the two were very close to each other and aligned with the target. You can also see that the advantage of adopting an external focus tended to increase with the relative difficulty of the task. With increasing speed of the target cursor *and* with increasing age of the participant, the difference between internal and external focus conditions became larger as well. These results provide preliminary evidence that adopting an external focus can be effective even for elderly persons—or perhaps particularly for this group, for whom many tasks become more challenging.

PARKINSON'S DISEASE

A few researchers have begun to examine whether instructions to adopt an external focus can enhance balance in individuals with Parkinson's disease (PD). As pointed out at the beginning of this chapter, balance problems and the associated risk of falling are major issues for those affected by PD. If balance training with an external focus could be shown to improve balance in persons with PD, this would have important implications for the design of physical therapy interventions. It would suggest that simple changes in the wording of instructions given to patients could enhance the effectiveness of balance training, presumably reducing the risk of falls and injuries. This, in turn, could reduce the time and costs of physical therapy interventions and, perhaps even more importantly, enhance the patients' quality of life. In this way, the payoff from a relatively simple manipulation of instructions during training could be substantial.

In one study that involved persons with PD, Canning (2005) examined how directing attention affected their gait when they were carrying a tray with glasses on it. Specifically, Canning instructed her participants to either focus on "maintaining big steps while walking" or on "balancing the tray and glasses." She found that when participants focused on walking, they walked faster and with longer strides compared to what happened in a baseline condition, in which they were not given focus instructions, and compared to what happened when they focused on the tray and glasses. In contrast, when participants focused on balancing the tray and glasses, they walked more slowly and with shorter strides than under baseline conditions. Canning argued that the instructions she gave not only directed attention to one task (walking) or the other (carrying the tray), but also induced an internal focus (walking) or an external focus (carrying the tray). Because the former type of attentional focus increased walking speed while the latter type of focus degraded it, she concluded that "the general suggestion that directing learners' attention to the effects of their movements be incorporated into rehabilitation practice . . . may not be appropriate in all circumstances for people with PD." (p. 98)

We certainly need more research in order to be able to make suggestions for the treatment of people with PD with confidence. But does Canning's finding indeed indicate that an internal focus might be more effective for people with PD? At first sight, one might be tempted to agree with this conclusion. However, there are problems with this interpretation. First, how do we know what exactly participants focused on when they were instructed to walk with "big steps"? Did they consciously control their leg movements to produce big steps (internal), or did they simply focus on covering a longer distance with each step (external)? Furthermore, what did they direct their attention to when asked to focus on balancing the tray and glasses? Did they focus on the glasses on the tray (external), or did they try to keep their hands still (internal)? The answer: We don't know. We cannot be sure how participants interpreted the instructions and whether the instruction induced an internal or external focus on either task. Second, the type of focus—assuming that it actually did differ between tasks—was confounded with the task (walking vs. carrying the tray). A "fair" comparison would have involved an external versus internal focus on either the postural task (walking) or the suprapostural task (carrying the tray), or on both tasks (as in the study by Wulf, Mercer, McNevin, & Guadagnoli, 2004). The only thing that Canning's (2005) study shows is that participants followed the instructions and performed more effectively on the task they were instructed to concentrate on—the walking task when they were instructed to focus on walking, and carrying the tray when they were instructed to focus on carrying the tray.

In another study, my colleagues and I explored the generalizability of the attentional focus effects to persons with PD (Landers et al., 2005). Specifically, we wanted to determine whether balance in individuals who have PD and a history of falls could be improved by giving them external focus instructions, relative to internal focus or no attentional focus instructions (control condition). For this experiment, we use a NeuroCom Smart Balance Master system (see photo). This system measures postural sway while the participant is standing still, and is designed to quantify an individual's ability to maintain balance under a variety of conditions. We tested our participants with an average age of 72.7 years under three conditions (in each of three attentional focus conditions, which are described in the next paragraph): eyes open, eyes closed, and a so-called sway-referenced condition with eyes open. In the latter condition, the support platform and the walls surrounding the participant move in accordance with the participant's movements. For example, if the participant leans forward, the platform and walls tilt forward as well, thereby minimizing the proprioceptive and visual feedback that would normally inform the person about his or her movement. This condition is very challenging, particularly for people whose balance is already compromised.

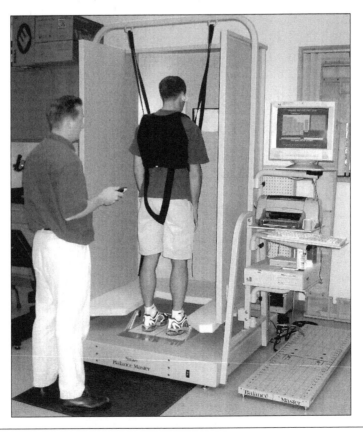

Participant on the Balance Master.

Under all conditions, participants stood on rectangular pieces of contact paper, one under each foot, that were placed on the platform. In the external focus condition, we instructed participants to concentrate on putting an equal amount of pressure on the rectangles, whereas in the internal focus condition we asked them to concentrate on putting an equal amount of pressure on their feet. In the control condition, they were simply asked to stand still.

The equilibrium scores for each condition are shown in figure 7.2. Even though there were no attentional focus differences for the two "easy" conditions (eyes open, eyes closed on the stable support surface), benefits of an external focus did emerge under the sway-referenced condition. Instructing participants to focus on the rectangles under their feet resulted in greater stability than instructing them to focus on the feet or not giving them any focus instructions. Also, as in previous studies, internal focus and control conditions produced similar scores. Furthermore, during the sway-referenced condition, several "falls" occurred under both internal focus and control conditions, but not under the external focus condition. ("Falls" are instances in which a participant completely lost his or her balance

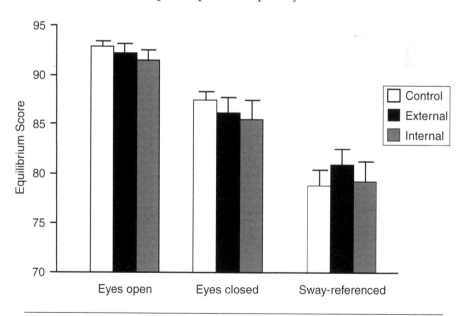

FIGURE 7.2 Equilibrium scores expressed as a percentage between 0 and 100, with 100 indicating perfect stability (small postural sway).

Reprinted from *Physiotherapy*, vol. 91, M. Landers, G. Wulf et al., "An external focus of attention attenuates balance impairment in Parkinson's disease," pgs. 152-185. Copyright 2005, with permission from Chartered Society of Physiotherapy.

and had to be supported by the harness that was being worn.) Thus, when the task was challenging enough (see also chapters 4 and 5), the benefits of an external focus were seen.

The findings of another study corroborate this conclusion (Wulf, Landers, & Töllner, 2006). In that study, we asked individuals with PD to stand on an inflated rubber disk (see figure 5.3). This is also a very difficult task for persons with PD. When participants were asked to focus on moving the disk as little as possible (external focus), their postural sway was significantly reduced compared to when they were asked to move their feet as little as possible (internal focus) or were not given attentional focus instructions (control). The results of both studies provide converging evidence that attentional focus effects generalize to individuals with PD. The findings might have practical implications for the clinic, as instructions given by physiotherapists often refer to the patient's movement coordination; that is, phrasing instructions so as to induce an external focus might enhance the effectiveness of training.

STROKE

Every 45 s, someone in the United States has a stroke, and every 3 min, someone dies of a stroke. People, who are lucky enough to survive often suffer from the consequences, which include paralysis, spasticity, balance problems, or speech and language problems. Often, fine motor skills are affected, such as use of the fingers to pick up an object. Physical and occupational therapists often work with people after stroke to practice these skills. In fact, people who had a stroke constitute the largest group of patients who are treated in occupational therapy (Trombly, 1995).

An important concept in occupational therapy that is reminiscent of the external focus manipulation is "purposeful activity" (Huss, 1981; King, 1978). Adding a purpose or functional relevance to a task has generally been found to enhance motor performance as compared to simulated activity or exercise with a focus on movement coordination (e.g., Lang, Nelson, & Bush, 1992; Steinbeck, 1986; Yoder, Nelson, & Smith, 1989; Wu, Trombly, & Lin, 1994; Wu et al., 1998). For example, Wu and colleagues (1998) found that having poststroke participants chop a mushroom with a real chopper produced more efficient, more direct, and smoother movements than having them use a simulated chopper. Similarly, when participants were asked to pick up a pencil from a pencil holder and prepare to write their names, their performance was more effective than that of participants who only pretended to perform the same movement, or that of participants who were instructed to simply reach forward (Wu, Trombly, & Lin, 1994). Wu and colleagues (1994) speculated that this advantage might be attributable to the fact that participants focused on the pencil, as opposed to focusing on the movement process. Other occupational therapists have also suggested that motor performance is facilitated when attention is directed to the goal rather than the movements themselves (Huss, 1981; King, 1978).

The interpretation that purposeful activity induces an external focus, whereas simulated activity promotes an internal focus, seems obvious. While attentional focus may indeed play a role in the differential effectiveness of purposeful versus simulated activity, there is also an important difference between the two approaches. Purposeful activity involves the use of objects whereas simulated activity does not. Of course, the use of real objects could also be a reason for the enhanced performance. An interesting question is therefore whether the attentional focus per se might have an effect on motor performance (and learning) in people who have experienced a stroke or cerebrovascular accident (CVA).

Given the beneficial effects of external focus instructions found for people without neurological impairments, Fasoli and colleagues set out to investigate the effects of external versus internal focus instructions in patients who had had a CVA (Fasoli et al., 2002). Because verbal instructions are frequently used in occupational therapy settings, Fasoli and colleagues argued that, if similar effects were found in that population, the implications for the effectiveness of the treatment might be important. They therefore used stroke patients and nonimpaired control participants to examine how the type of focus affected the performance of daily-life tasks. The tasks included "(a) removing a can from a shelf and placing it on a table, (b) taking an apple off a shelf and putting it into a basket, and (c) moving an empty coffee mug from a table onto a saucer" (p. 382). The instructions directed participants' attention either to the object they were to manipulate or to the control of their movements. For example, for the first task, in the external focus condition, the instructions were "Pay attention to the can: Think about where it is on the shelf and how big or heavy it is." The internal focus instructions for the same task were "Pay attention to your arm: Think about how much you straighten your elbow and how your wrist and fingers move" (p. 383). All participants performed all tasks under both external and internal focus conditions, with the order of tasks being counterbalanced between participants.

The results showed that both impaired and nonimpaired groups performed the tasks more effectively if given external rather than internal focus instructions. Specifically, movement times were shorter and peak velocities were greater on all tasks. This suggests that participants with stroke and control participants preplanned their movements to a greater extent and used more automatic control processes when they focused externally. Fasoli and colleagues (2005) concluded, "The results support the use of externally focused instruction directed toward naturalistic task performance to improve movement speed and force in the hemiparetic arm after stroke. This research reinforces the need for therapists to consider their use of instructions when evaluating and treating movement disorders after stroke" (p. 388).

SPEECH DISORDERS

Speech disorders are another area in which the use of external focus instructions might make therapeutic intervention more effective. One common speech disorder is apraxia (or dyspraxia). Persons with apraxia have trouble saying what they want to say correctly and consistently. They have difficulty putting sounds and syllables together in the correct order to form words. Also, long and more complex words are usually harder for them to pronounce than short and simple words. Whereas acquired apraxia of speech typically occurs in adults and is caused by damage to the parts of the brain involved in speaking (e.g., resulting from a stroke, head injury, or tumor), developmental apraxia of speech occurs in children and is present from birth. The causes of this disorder in children are not yet known.

Regardless of the person's age or the cause of the disorder, speech therapy typically involves instructions that direct the patient's attention to the articulators, such as the tongue or lips (e.g., phonetic placement therapy). An interesting question is therefore, Would instructions that induced an external focus be beneficial for speech treatment of individuals with motor speech disorders, including apraxia of speech? Skott Freedman, a doctoral student in Language and Communicative Disorders at San Diego State University, has begun to examine this issue. In his first study, he used an oral-motor task to see whether attentional focus effects would be found for this type of task (Freedman et al., in press). He argued that if external focus advantages were found for a task using the oral-motor system, this might have implications for the therapy of speech disorders. Follow-up studies could then be conducted to determine the generalizability to patient populations and the skills they attempt to learn in speech therapy.

In Freedman's study, healthy undergraduate students practiced a task that required them to produce rapid pressure bursts to a target level of 20% of their maximal strength. This task was performed with either the hand (to try to replicate earlier findings related to limb movements) or the tongue (to examine the generalizability of those findings to the oral-motor system). The pressure was exerted against a rubber bulb that participants had in their hand or in their mouth. Visual concurrent feedback was presented on a computer screen on each trial. Participants were to apply only enough pressure in a rapid exertion to see their pressure burst appear in a 20% target window slot. Participants who were assigned to the internal focus group were instructed to focus on the pressure exerted with their hand or tongue, whereas those in the external group were instructed to focus on the pressure exerted on the bulb.

All participants became generally more accurate at producing 20% of their maximum force with either the hand or the tongue across practice. Importantly, participants who were given external focus instructions were overall more accurate (and less variable) than those who were given internal focus instructions. This was the case for both hand and tongue. This finding demonstrates that the external focus advantages indeed generalize to the oral-motor system. It suggests that attentional focus may also be a critical variable in speech treatments. If similar external focus advantages were found for more speech-related tasks and for people with speech or voice disorders, there might be important implications for speech treatment. Through the design of instructions, feedback, or perhaps exercises so that they direct attention externally, rather than internally, speech therapy might become more effective.

ATTENTIONAL INSIGHTS

Dr. Geralyn Schulz is a professor and chair of the Department of Speech and Hearing Science at George Washington University. She has published extensively on speech motor learning. Here she shares some of her clinical experience with speech therapy, and, in particular, the effectiveness of different attentional foci.

Speech language pathologists provide rehabilitation services to persons who have an impairment in the ability to communicate due to developmental and/or acquired disorders. The ability to produce speech is estimated to be impaired in approximately 5 million Americans as the result of neurologic insult from strokes, traumatic brain injury and Parkinson's disease. There are millions more whose ability to accurately produce speech is affected by the numerous other developmental and acquired disorders that exist. Typically, speech pathologists utilize general strategies to promote improved production of specific sounds by focusing on articulatory-kinematic aspects of sound production with such techniques as articulatory placement cues (e.g., verbal articulatory placement instructions, having patients look at photos or drawings of where the tongue would be placed for a certain sound, use of a mirror to aid in the physical placement of the lips and jaw, clinician manually guiding client articulators to appropriate positions to produce sounds, etc.), phonetic derivation (which starts with a single sound then gradually builds to words and phrases), integral stimulation (clinician instructs client to 'Watch me, listen to me, and say it with me.'), and practice of phonemic contrasts (e.g., alternating productions between words that differ in only one sound such as zip and sip). Such therapy techniques can be grouped together by their 'internal focus'; that is, they focus on having the client place their articulators in various positions and rely primarily on the adequacy of auditory feedback to shape articulatory movements of the tongue, lips, jaw, and soft palate. While the majority of treatment studies that are available have demonstrated increased abilities in speech production for specific treatment targets, evidence for generalization and maintenance of treatment gains is predominantly lacking. That is, those sounds or words or sentences that are treated in therapy improve but the improvement does not generalize to other nontrained sounds or words or sentences and what improvement is observed is not long lasting and the production regresses. In addition, treatment techniques that may be effective for one client or one type of neurogenic speech disorder do not necessarily generalize to other clients with the same disorder or to clients with other types of neurogenic speech disorders. I believe that this lack of sustained improvement is due, at least in significant part, to the internal focus of the therapy techniques. Consider the situation in adult speech remediation: adults have been speaking for 20+ years without ever thinking about *where* they are placing or moving their lips, tongue, jaw, and palate. They think about *what* they want to say perhaps but rarely about *how* they need to move to make the sounds that make up the words which express their thoughts. Suddenly, when they acquire a disorder that results in speech articulation problems, a speech language pathologist is having them think about *where and how* they are moving their tongue, lips, jaw, and palate (not to mention the respiratory system, the vocal cords, the larynx, the pharynx, etc). It is not surprising to me that our therapy techniques are as ineffective as they are, and in fact I am sometimes surprised they work as well as they do. In my experience and in the literature that does exist, those therapy techniques that have a more 'external focus' appear to have the most benefit. That is, those therapy techniques that take the focus away from the where and how the movement is made by the client and place it more on the results of the movement. For example, therapy techniques that involve visual feedback that the client can imitate often work much better than the instructions to 'put your tongue here, then move it there while at the same time opening your vocal folds slightly and closing your lips' to say 'ta'. Working with a large mirror in which the client can see the therapist's facial movements as well as their own often results in better and longer lasting improvement in articulation of sounds that can be visualized outside the oral cavity. Being able to visualize the movement of one's own soft palate (velum) during speech has been proven efficacious in establishing and promoting con-

(continued)

sistent closure of the oro-nasal port (necessary for all speech sounds in English except 'm', 'n' and 'ng') in patients who had pharyngeal surgery. Another example of the difference in focus during speech therapy comes from techniques that target intonation and stress placement. An internal focus would have the client raise the pitch of their voice, increase the intensity and prolong slightly the word in the sentence that is to receive stress. An external focus would have the client respond to questions such as the following (with the prior knowledge that the client's car is a blue Volvo): Clinician question: 'The car you are driving is red?' Client responds, 'No, the car I drive is BLUE.' Clinician question: 'The Chevy you are driving is blue?' Client responds: 'No, I drive a VOLVO.' Or 'No, the VOLVO I drive is blue.' Without fail, I have had clients automatically raise the pitch of their voice, increase the intensity and prolong slightly the word that should receive the stress. Yet another example is for the client who has difficulty controlling the intonation pattern of a falling intonation that in English marks the end of a declarative statement but also marks the end of a clause or the end of a thought. These clients tend to have either a flat intonation pattern (which signals to the listener that the thought is not complete and they should wait or which makes it difficult to 'chunk' the acoustic signal to quickly decipher the meaning of the utterance) or a raising intonation pattern (which signals to the listener that a question was asked). An internal rehabilitation focus would have the client lower his pitch and slightly prolong the last word/syllable. A more externally focused approach would be to have the client slightly nod his/her head at the end of an utterance/sentence. This in effect shortens the vocal cords, which automatically reduces the pitch of your voice. You can try this out for yourself and see how well it works by holding an 'ah' sound while moving your head up and down. The point is that the focus is away from what the client is actually doing to make the articulators actually move to produce the desired result and toward the goal of the movement.

SUMMARY

A few studies have begun to examine attentional focus effects on motor performance in children, in persons who are elderly, and in those with conditions that affect the motor system, such as PD or stroke. Even though learning effects were not examined, the results of these studies suggest that instructions to adopt an external focus can improve motor performance in these populations as well. Tracking (in people who are elderly), balance (in children and persons with PD), and the performance of various tasks involving reaching and grasping (in individuals who have had a stroke) benefited from those instructions. Finally, preliminary evidence that the attentional focus effects generalize to the oral-motor system is encouraging, as it suggests that speech therapists might be able to enhance the effectiveness of their interventions by taking advantage of this effect. Further studies are needed that address the long-term effects of attentional focus manipulations in patient populations.

PRACTICAL APPLICATIONS

EXAMPLES OF EXTERNAL FOCUS

In physical or occupational therapy settings, therapists often give patients instructions or feedback that is specifically intended to direct their attention to the details of how they execute certain movements. Based on the findings reviewed in this chapter, the effectiveness of interventions might be enhanced if patients were encouraged to adopt an external focus. For example, a metronome or music has been used effectively during gait training in persons with neurological disorders. When patients are instructed to move in time with the music or metronome, they are encouraged to modify their gait pattern without conscious intervention into the control processes. If the task involves negotiating obstacles, instructing people to focus on the height of the obstacle they are stepping over might lead to better performance than instructing them to focus on lifting the foot high enough (McNevin, Wulf, & Calson, 2000).

- During gait training a therapist could instruct a stroke patient to imagine (or perform) kicking a ball at the end of the swing phase, rather than asking her to focus on her heel strikes. How might the image of kicking a ball help to improve a patient's gait pattern?

- What are other examples of how "typical" instructions in physical therapy might be modified to enhance the rehabilitation process?

ADDITIONAL RESOURCES

Instructing patients to adopt an external focus while performing certain tasks might not only allow the behavior to be controlled more automatically; it might have the additional advantage that it frees up attentional resources (see chapter 4) that could be directed toward other environmental cues (e.g., uneven ground, other pedestrians, traffic). As pointed out by Guadagnoli, McNevin, and Wulf (2002), "[M]any intervention strategies encourage individuals to 'watch their step' or simply to avoid situations that may pose a challenge to balance integrity. Neither situation is likely to promote functional recovery and at worst, may actually lead to further impairment" (p. 138). Encouraging people with balance problems to adopt an external focus of attention might enhance their balance *and* facilitate their interactions with the environment.

- Think of a situation that might pose a challenge to an individual who is at risk for falls and consider the types of instructions you would give this individual.

FUTURE DIRECTIONS

GENERALIZABILITY TO OTHER POPULATIONS

Few studies have addressed attentional focus effects in populations other than young, healthy adults. While some studies have looked at the effects in people who are elderly and in persons with PD or stroke, it would be interesting to see whether the external focus advantages generalize to other patient populations with motor impairments, such as those with cerebral palsy or incomplete spinal cord injury. In addition, it would be important to examine long-term effects of attentional focus training, as well as the transferability of practiced skills to novel situations, as real-life situations are seldom identical to those encountered in rehabilitation settings. If the effectiveness of clinical interventions could be enhanced by a simple change in the wording of instructions or feedback, the potential benefits might include shorter rehabilitation phases, perhaps fewer falls or injuries, and an enhanced quality of life for the patient.

Finally, even though some researchers have begun to examine attentional focus effects in children, more studies are needed to determine the age at which those effects begin to manifest themselves. Very young children might not have the attention span or attentional capacity to follow instructions while performing a motor skill. Alternatively, they might have a natural propensity to focus on the outcome of their actions, making external focus instructions essentially redundant. Future studies should determine at what age attentional focus instructions might be used effectively.

REFERENCES

Abernethy, B. (1988). Dual-task methodology and motor skills research: Some applications and methodological constraints. *Journal of Human Movement Studies, 14,* 101-132.

Adams, J.A. (1971). A closed-loop theory of motor learning. *Journal of Motor Behavior, 3,* 111-150.

Al-Abood, S.A., Bennett, S.J., Hernandez, F.M., Ashford, D., & Davids, K. (2002). Effects of verbal instructions and image size on visual search strategies in basketball free throw shooting. *Journal of Sports Sciences, 20,* 271-278.

Balasubramaniam, R., & Turvey, M.T. (2000). The handedness of postural fluctuations. *Human Movement Science, 19,* 667-684.

Barth, C. (2005). Externer Fokus [External focus]. Paper presented at Physiokongress, Aachen, Germany, May 5-7.

Bauer, G. (2001). *Lehrbuch Fussball [Textbook soccer]* (6th ed.). München: BLV.

Baumeister, R.F. (1984). Choking under pressure: Self-consciousness and paradoxical effects of incentives on skillful performance. *Journal of Personality and Social Psychology, 46,* 610-620.

Baumeister, R.F. (1985). The championship choke. *Psychology Today* (April), 48-53.

Baumeister, R.F., & Showers, C.J. (1986). A review of paradoxical performance effects: Choking under pressure in sports and mental test. *European Journal for Social Psychology, 16,* 361-383.

Baumeister, R.F., & Steinhilber, A. (1984). Paradoxical effects of supportive audiences in performance under pressure: The home field advantage in sport championships. *Journal of Personality and Social Psychology, 47,* 85-93.

Beilock, S.L., Bertenthal, B.I., McCoy, A.M., & Carr, T.H. (2004). Haste does not always make waste: Expertise, direction of attention, and speed versus accuracy in performing sensorimotor skills. *Psychonomic Bulletin and Review, 11,* 373-379.

Beilock, S.L., & Carr, T.H. (2001). On the fragility of skilled performance: What governs choking under pressure? *Journal of Experimental Psychology: General, 130,* 701-725.

Beilock, S.L., & Carr, T.H. (2004). From novice to expert performance: Defining the path to excellence. In A.M. Williams & N.J. Hodges (Eds.), *Skill acquisition in sport: Research, theory and practice* (pp. 309-327). London: Routledge.

Beilock, S.L., Carr, T.H., MacMahon, C., & Starkes, J.L. (2002). When paying attention becomes counterproductive: Impact of divided versus skill-focused attention on novice and experienced performance of sensorimotor skills. *Journal of Experimental Psychology: Applied, 8,* 6-16.

Bernstein, N.A. (1967). *The co-ordination and regulation of movements.* Oxford: Pergamon Press.

Beuter, A., & Duda, J.L. (1985). Analysis of the arousal/motor performance relationship in children using movement kinematics. *Journal of Sport Psychology, 7,* 229-243.

Bilodeau, E.A., & Bilodeau, I.M. (1958). Variable frequency of knowledge of results and the learning of a simple skill. *Journal of Experimental Psychology, 55,* 379-383.

Bilodeau, E.A., Bilodeau, I.M., & Schumsky, D.A. (1959). Some effects of introducing and withdrawing knowledge of results early and late in practice. *Journal of Experimental Psychology, 58,* 142-144.

Boyce, B.A. (1992). Effects of assigned versus participant-set goals on skill acquisition and retention of a selected shooting task. *Journal of Teaching in Physical Education, 11,* 220-234.

Burton, D. (1994). Goal setting in sport. In R.N. Singer, M. Murphey, & L.K. Tennant (Eds.), *Handbook of research on sport psychology* (pp. 467-491). New York: Macmillan.

Canning, C.G. (2005). The effect of directing attention during walking under dual-task conditions in Parkinson's disease. *Parkinsonism and Related Disorders, 11,* 95-99.

Castaneda, B., & Gray, R. (in press). Effects of focus of attention on baseball batting performance in expert and novice players. *Journal of Sport and Exercise Psychology.*

Csikszentmihalyi, M. (1990). *Flow: The psychology of optimal experience.* New York: Harper & Row.

Easterbrook, J.A. (1959). The effect of emotion on cue utilization and the organization of behavior. *Psychological Review, 66,* 183-201.

Fasoli, S.E., Trombly, C.A., Tickle-Degnen, L., & Verfaellie, M.H. (2002). Effect of instructions on functional reach in persons with and without cerebrovascular accident. *American Journal of Occupational Therapy, 56,* 380-390.

Fitts, P.M. (1964). Perceptual-motor skills learning. In A.W. Melton (Ed.), *Categories of human learning* (pp. 243-285). New York: Academic Press.

Fitts, P.M., & Posner, M.I.. (1967). *Human performance*. Belmont, CA: Brooks/Cole.

Ford, P., Hodges, N.J., & Williams, A.M. (2005). On-line attentional-focus manipulations in a soccer dribbling task: Implications for the proceduralization of motor skills. *Journal of Motor Behavior, 37*, 386-394.

Freedman, S., Maas, E., Wulf, G., Caligiuiri, M., & Robin, D. (in press). Effects of attentional focus on oral-motor control and learning. *Journal of Speech, Language, and Hearing Research.*

Gallwey, W.T. (1982). *The inner game of tennis*. New York: Bantam Books.

Gantert, C., Honerkamp, J., & Timmer, J. (1992). Analyzing the dynamics of hand tremor time series. *Biological Cybernetics, 66*, 479-484.

Garfield, C.A., & Bennett, H.A. (1985). *Peak performance: Mental training techniques of the world's greatest athletes*. Los Angeles: Tarcher.

Gentile, A.M. (1987). Skill acquisition: Action, movement and neuromotor processes. In J. Carr & R. Shepherd (Eds.), *Movement science: Foundations for physical therapy in rehabilitation*. Rockville, MD: Aspen.

Gentile, A.M. (1998). Implicit and explicit processes during acquisition of functional skills. *Scandinavian Journal of Occupational Therapy, 5*, 7-16.

Gray, R. (2004). Attending to the execution of a complex sensorimotor skill: Expertise differences, choking, and slumps. *Journal of Experimental Psychology: Applied, 10*, 42-54.

Guadagnoli, M.A., McNevin, N., & Wulf, G. (2002). Cognition influences to balance and posture. *Orthopaedic Physical Therapy Clinics of North America, 11*, 131-141.

Hardy, L., Mullen, R., & Jones, G. (1996). Knowledge and conscious control of motor actions under stress. *British Journal of Psychology, 87*, 621-636.

Hebert, E.P., & Landin, D. (1994). Effects of a learning model and augmented feedback on tennis skill acquisition. *Research Quarterly for Exercise and Sport, 65*, 250-257.

Hodges, N.J., & Franks, I.M. (2001). Learning a coordination skill: Interactive effects of instruction and feedback. *Research Quarterly for Exercise and Sport, 72*, 132-142.

Hodges, N.J., & Lee, T.D. (1999). The role of augmented information prior to learning a bimanual visual-motor coordination task: Do instructions of the movement pattern facilitate learning relative to discovery learning? *British Journal of Psychology, 90*, 389-403.

Hollmann, W., & Hettinger, T. (2000). *Sportmedizin Grundlagen für Arbeit, Training und Präventivmedizin [Sports medicine fundamentals for work, exercise, and preventative medicine]* (4th ed.). Stuttgart, New York: Schattauer-Verlag.

Hoppe, D., Sadakata, M., & Desain, P. (2006). Development of real-time visual feedback, assistance in singing training: A review. *Journal of Computer Assisted Learning, 22,* 308-316.

Huss, A.J. (1981). From kinesiology to adaptation. *American Journal of Occupational Therapy, 35,* 574-580.

Kim, J., Singer, R.N., & Radlo, S.J. (1996). Degree of cognitive demand in psychomotor tasks and the effects of the Five-Step Strategy on achievement. *Human Performance, 9,* 155-169.

King, L.J. (1978). Toward a science of adaptive responses. *American Journal of Occupational Therapy, 32,* 429-437.

Koller, W.C., Glatt, S., Vetere-Overfield, B., & Hassanein, R. (1989). Falls and Parkinson's disease. *Clinical Neuropharmacology, 12,* 98-105.

Kyllo, L.B., & Landers, D.M. (1995). Goal setting in sport and exercise: A research synthesis to resolve the controversy. *Journal of Sport and Exercise Psychology, 17,* 117-137.

Lai, Q., & Shea, C.H. (1998). Generalized motor program (GMP) learning: Effects of reduced frequency of knowledge of results and practice variability. *Journal of Motor Behavior, 30,* 51-59.

Landers, M., Wulf, G., Wallmann, H., & Guadagnoli, M.A. (2005). An external focus of attention attenuates balance impairment in Parkinson's disease. *Physiotherapy, 91,* 152-185.

Lang, E.M., Nelson, D.L., & Bush, M.A. (1992). Comparison of performance in materials-based occupation, imagery-based occupation, and rote exercise in nursing home residents. *American Journal of Occupational Therapy, 46,* 607-611.

Leavitt, J.L. (1979). Cognitive demands of skating and stickhandling in ice hockey. *Canadian Journal of Applied Sports Science, 4,* 46-55.

Lewis, B.P., & Linder, D.E. (1997). Thinking about choking? Attentional processes and paradoxical performance. *Personality and Social Psychology Bulletin, 23,* 937-944.

Liao, C.M., & Master, R.S.W. (2002). Self-focused attention and performance failure under psychological stress. *Journal of Sport and Exercise Psychology, 24,* 289-305.

Maddox, M.D., Wulf, G., & Wright, D.L. (1999). The effects of an internal vs. external focus of attention on the learning of a tennis stroke. *Journal of Exercise Psychology, 21,* S78.

Magill, R.A., Chamberlin, C.J., & Hall, K.G. (1991). Verbal knowledge of results as redundant information for learning an anticipation timing skill. *Human Movement Science, 10,* 485-507.

Marchant, D., Clough, P.J., & Crawshaw, M. (in press). The effects of attentional focusing strategies on novice dart throwing performances and their experiences. *International Journal of Sport and Exercise Psychology*.

Marchant, D., Greig, M., Scott, C., & Clough, P. (2006). Attentional focusing strategies influence muscle activity during isokinetic bicep curls. Poster presented at the annual conference of the British Psychological Society, Cardiff, UK.

Masters, R.S.W. (1992). Knowledge, knerves and know-how: The role of explicit versus implicit knowledge in the breakdown of a complex motor skill under pressure. *British Journal of Psychology, 83*, 343-358.

Masters, R.S.W. (2000). Theoretical aspects of implicit learning in sport. *International Journal of Sport Psychology, 31*, 530-541.

Masters, R.S.W., Polman, R.C.J., & Hammond, N.V. (1993). "Reinvestment": A dimension of personality implicated in skill breakdown under pressure. *Personality and Individual Differences, 14*, 655-666.

Maxwell, J.P., Masters, R.S.W., & Eves, F.F. (2000). From novice to no know-how: A longitudinal study of implicit motor learning. *Journal of Sports Sciences, 18*, 111-120.

McCullagh, P., & Meyer, K.N. (1997). Learning versus correct models: Influence of model type on the learning of a free-weight squat lift. *Research Quarterly for Exercise and Sport, 68*, 56-61.

McCullagh, P., & Weiss, M. (2001). Modeling: Considerations for motor skill performance and psychological responses. In R.N. Singer, H.A. Hausenblas, & C.M. Janelle (Eds.), *Handbook of sport psychology* (pp. 205-238). New York: Wiley.

McNevin, N.H., Shea, C.H., & Wulf, G. (2003). Increasing the distance of an external focus of attention enhances learning. *Psychological Research, 67*, 22-29.

McNevin, N.H., & Wulf, G. (2002). Attentional focus on supra-postural tasks affects postural control. *Human Movement Science, 21*, 187-202.

McNevin, N.H., Wulf, G., & Carlson, C. (2000). Effects of attentional focus, self-control, and dyad training effects on motor learning: Implications for physical rehabilitation. *Physical Therapy, 80*, 373-385.

Mechsner, F. (2004). A psychological approach to human voluntary movements. *Journal of Motor Behavior, 36*, 355-370.

Mechsner, F., Kerzel, D., Knoblich, G., & Prinz, W. (2001). Perceptual basis of bimanual coordination. *Nature, 414*, 69-73.

Meinel, K., & Schnabel, G. (1976). *Bewegungslehre [Movement science]*. Berlin: Sportverlag.

Newell, K.M., Gao, F., & Sprague, R.L. (1995). The dynamics of finger tremor in tardive dyskinesia. *Chaos, 5,* 43-47.

Nicholson, D.E., & Schmidt, R.A. (1991). Scheduling information feedback to enhance training effectiveness. *Proceedings of the Human Factors Society 35th annual meeting* (pp. 1400-1403). Santa Monica, CA: Human Factors Society.

Park, J-H., Shea, C.H., McNevin, N.H., & Wulf, G. (2000). Attentional focus and the control of dynamic balance. *Journal of Sport and Exercise Psychology, 22,* S85.

Park, J-H., Shea, C.H., & Wright, D.L. (2000). Reduced frequency concurrent and terminal feedback: A test of the guidance hypothesis. *Journal of Motor Behavior, 32,* 287-296.

Perkins-Ceccato, N., Passmore, S.R., & Lee, T.D. (2003). Effects of focus of attention depend on golfers' skill. *Journal of Sports Sciences, 21,* 593-600.

Pijpers, J.J., Oudejans, R.R., & Bakker, F.C. (2005). Anxiety-induced changes in movement behaviour during the execution of a complex whole-body task. *Quarterly Journal of Experimental Psychology, 58A,* 421-445.

Poolton, J., Maxwell, J.P., Masters, R.S.W., & Raab, M. (2006). Benefits of an external focus of attention: Common coding or conscious processing? *Journal of Sport Sciences, 24,* 89-99.

Riley, M.A., Stoffregen, T.A., Grocki, M.J., & Turvey, M.T. (1999). Postural stabilization for the control of touching. *Human Movement Science, 18,* 795-817.

Rougier, P. (2003). Visual feedback induces opposite effects on elementary centre of gravity and centre of pressure minus centre of gravity motions in undisturbed upright stance. *Clinical Biomechanics, 18,* 341-349.

Salmoni, A.W., Schmidt, R.A., & Walter, C.B. (1984). Knowledge of results and motor learning: A review and critical appraisal. *Psychological Bulletin, 95,* 355-386.

Saxer, M. (2004). "Mit schwimmenden Schultern"—Zur Optimierung motorischer Automatisierungsprozesse durch Spiel- und Übeanweisungen ["With floating shoulders"—optimizing the automatization of motor processes through instructions for playing and practicing]. *Üben & Musizieren, 3,* 6-11.

Schmidt, R.A. (1975). A schema theory of discrete motor skill learning. *Psychological Review, 82,* 225-260.

Schmidt, R.A. (1991). Frequent augmented feedback can degrade learning: Evidence and interpretations. In J. Requin & G.E. Stelmach (Eds.), *Tutorials in motor neuroscience* (pp. 59-75). Dordrecht, The Netherlands: Kluwer Academic.

Schmidt, R.A., & Lee, T.D. (2005). *Motor control and learning: A behavioral emphasis* (4th ed.). Champaign, IL: Human Kinetics.

Schmidt, R.A., & Wrisberg, C.A. (2004). *Motor learning and performance* (3rd ed.). Champaign, IL: Human Kinetics.

Schmidt, R.A., & Wulf, G. (1997). Continuous concurrent feedback degrades skill learning: Implications for training and simulation. *Human Factors, 39,* 509-525.

Schneider, W., & Fisk, A.D. (1983). Attention theory and mechanisms for skilled performance. In R.A. Magill (Ed.), *Memory and control of action* (pp. 119-143). Amsterdam: North-Holland.

Shea, C.H., Wright, D.L., Wulf, G., & Whitacre, C. (2000). Physical and observational practice afford unique learning opportunities. *Journal of Motor Behavior, 32,* 27-36.

Shea, C.H., & Wulf, G. (1999). Enhancing motor learning through external-focus instructions and feedback. *Human Movement Science, 18,* 553-571.

Shea, C.H., Wulf, G., & Whitacre, C.A. (1999). Enhancing training efficiency and effectiveness through the use of dyad training. *Journal of Motor Behavior, 31,* 119-125.

Singer, R.N. (1985). Sport performance: A five-step mental approach. *Journal of Physical Education and Recreation, 57,* 82-84.

Singer, R.N. (1988). Strategies and metastrategies in learning and performing self-paced athletic skills. *Sport Psychologist, 2,* 49-68.

Singer, R.N., Cauraugh, J.H., Tennant, L.K., Murphey, M., Chen, D., & Lidor, R. (1991). Attention and distractors: Considerations for enhancing sport performances. *International Journal of Sport Psychology, 22,* 95-114.

Singer, R.N., Lidor, R., & Cauraugh, J.H. (1993). To be aware or not aware: What to think about while learning and performing a motor skill. *Sport Psychologist, 7,* 19-30.

Smith, M.D., & Chamberlin, C.J. (1992). Effect of adding cognitively demanding tasks on soccer skill performance. *Perceptual and Motor Skills, 75,* 955-961.

Steinbeck, T.M. (1986). Purposeful activity and performance. *American Journal of Occupational Therapy, 40,* 529-534.

Stoffregen, T.A., Pagualayan, R.J., Bardy, B.G., & Hettinger, L.J. (2000). Modulating postural control to facilitate visual performance. *Human Movement Science, 19,* 203-220.

Swinnen, S.P. (1996). Information feedback for motor skill learning: A review. In H.N. Zelaznik (Ed.), *Advances in motor learning and control* (pp. 37-66). Champaign, IL: Human Kinetics.

Thompson, J.M.T., & Stewart, H.B. (1986). *Nonlinear dynamics and chaos.* New York: Wiley.

Thorn, J. (2006). Using attentional strategies for balance performance and learning in nine through 12 year olds. Doctoral dissertation, Florida State University, Tallahassee.

Thorndike, E.L. (1914). *Educational psychology.* New York: Columbia University.

Thorndike, E.L. (1927). The law of effect. *American Journal of Psychology, 39,* 212-222.

Thorndike, E.L. (1932). *The fundamentals of learning.* New York: Teachers College.

Thuraisingam, A.I., Levine, D.F., & Andersen, J.T. (2006). Can research in sports and other motor skills help improve endoscopy training? *Gastrointestinal Endoscopy, 63,* 276-279.

Totsika, V., & Wulf, G. (2003). The influence of external and internal foci of attention on transfer to novel situations and skills. *Research Quarterly for Exercise and Sport, 74,* 220-225.

Tranter, L. (2001). Focus of attention and counter-intentional errors in a golf learning paradigm. Bachelor of Arts thesis, University of Reading, United Kingdom.

Trombly, C.A. (1995). *Occupational therapy for physical dysfunction* (4th ed.). Baltimore: Williams & Wilkins.

Vallacher, R.R. (1993). Mental calibration: Forging a working relationship between mind and action. In D.M. Wegner & J.W. Pennebaker (Eds.), *Handbook of mental control.* Englewood Cliffs, NJ: Prentice Hall.

Vallacher, R.R., & Wegner, D.M. (1987). What do people think they're doing? Action identification and human behavior. *Psychological Review, 94,* 3-15.

Vance, J., Wulf, G., Töllner, T., McNevin, N.H., & Mercer, J. (2004). EMG activity as a function of the performer's focus of attention. *Journal of Motor Behavior, 36,* 450-459.

Vander Linden, D.W., Cauraugh, J.H., & Greene, T.A. (1993). The effect of frequency of kinetic feedback on learning an isometric force production task in nondisabled subjects. *Physical Therapy, 73,* 79-87.

Vereijken, B. (1991). *The dynamics of skill acquisition.* Meppel, Netherlands: Krips Repro.

Vereijken, B., & Whiting, H.T.A. (1990). In defense of discovery learning. *Canadian Journal of Sport Science, 15,* 99-106.

Vereijken, B., Whiting, H.T.A., & Beek, W.J. (1992). A dynamical systems approach to skill acquisition. *Quarterly Journal of Experimental Psychology, 45A,* 323-344.

Vuillerme, N., & Nafati, G. (2005). How attentional focus on body sway affects postural control during quiet standing. *Psychological Research, 69,* 1-9.

Wan, C.Y., & Huon, G.F. (2005). Performance degradation under pressure in music: An examination of attentional processes. *Psychology of Music, 33,* 155-172.

Weeks, D.L., & Anderson, L.P. (2000). The interaction of observational learning with overt practice: Effects on motor skill learning. *Acta Psychologica, 104,* 259-271.

Weeks, D.L., & Kordus, R.N. (1998). Relative frequency of knowledge of performance and motor skill learning. *Research Quarterly for Exercise and Sport, 69,* 224-230.

Weinberg, R.S. (1978). The effects of success and failure on the patterning of neuromuscular energy. *Journal of Motor Behavior, 10,* 53-61.

Weinberg, R.S. (1994). Goal setting and performance in sport and exercise settings: A synthesis and critique. *Medicine and Science in Sports and Exercise, 26,* 469-477.

Weinberg, R.S., & Hunt, V.V. (1976). The relationship between anxiety, motor performance, and electromyography. *Journal of Motor Behavior, 8,* 219-224.

Weir, P., McNevin, N.H., Quinn, T., & Wulf, G. (2005). The effect of attentional focus and age on supra-postural task performance. Paper presented at the Annual Meeting of the *Canadian Society for Psychomotor Learning and Sport Psychology (SCAPPS)*. Niagara Falls, Canada.

Welch, G.F., Howard, D.M., Himonides, E., & Brereton, J. (2005). Real-time feedback in the singing studio: An innovatory action-research project using new voice technology. *Music Education Research, 7,* 225-249.

Welch, G.F., Rush, C., & Howard, D.M. (1989). Real-time visual feedback in the development of vocal pitch accuracy in singing. *Psychology of Music, 17,* 146-157.

Whiting, H.T.A., & Vereijken, B. (1993). The acquisition of coordination in skill learning. *International Journal of Sport Psychology, 24,* 343-357.

Whiting, H.T.A., Vogt, S., & Vereijken, B. (1992). Human skill and motor control: Some aspects of the motor control-motor learning relation. In J.J. Summers (Ed.), *Approaches to the study of motor control and learning*. Amsterdam: North-Holland.

Wine, J. (1971). Test anxiety and direction of attention. *Psychological Bulletin, 76,* 92-104.

Winstein, C.J., Pohl, P.S., Cardinale, C., Green, A., Scholtz, L., & Waters, C.S. (1996). Learning a partial-weight-bearing skill: Effectiveness of two forms of feedback. *Physical Therapy, 76,* 985-993.

Winstein, C.J., Pohl, P.S., & Lewthwaite, R. (1994). Effects of physical guidance and knowledge of results on motor learning: Support for the guidance hypothesis. *Research Quarterly for Exercise and Sport, 65,* 316-323.

Winstein, C.J., & Schmidt, R.A. (1990). Reduced frequency of knowledge of results enhances motor skill learning. *Journal of Experimental Psychology: Learning, Memory, and Cognition, 16,* 677-691.

Wrisberg, C.A., & Wulf, G. (1997). Diminishing the effects of reduced frequency of knowledge of results on generalized motor program learning. *Journal of Motor Behavior, 29,* 17-26.

Wu, C., Trombly, C.A., & Lin, K. (1994). The relationship between occupational form and occupational performance: A kinematic perspective. *American Journal of Occupational Therapy, 48,* 679-688.

Wu, C., Trombly, C.A., Lin, K., & Tickle-Degnen, L. (1998). Effects of object affordances on reaching performance in persons with and without cerebrovascular accident. *American Journal of Occupational Therapy, 52,* 447-456.

Wulf, G, & Su, J. (in press). An external focus of attention enhances golf shot accuracy in beginners and experts. *Research Quarterly for Exercise and Sport.*

Wulf, G. (2006). *Attentional focus effects in balance acrobats.* Manuscript submitted for publication.

Wulf, G., Eder, S., & Parma, J. (2005). Observational practice and attentional focus: Benefits of instructions inducing an external focus. Unpublished manuscript: University of Nevada, Las Vegas.

Wulf, G., Höβ, M., & Prinz, W. (1998). Instructions for motor learning: Differential effects of internal versus external focus of attention. *Journal of Motor Behavior, 30,* 169-179.

Wulf, G., Landers, M., & Töllner, T. (2006). *Postural instability in Parkinson's disease decreases with an external focus of attention.* Manuscript submitted for publication.

Wulf, G., Lauterbach, B., & Toole, T. (1999). Learning advantages of an external focus of attention in golf. *Research Quarterly for Exercise and Sport, 70,* 120-126.

Wulf, G., Lee, T.D., & Schmidt, R.A. (1994). Reducing knowledge of results about relative versus absolute timing: Differential effects on learning. *Journal of Motor Behavior, 26,* 362-369.

Wulf, G., McConnel, N., Gärtner, M., & Schwarz, A. (2002). Feedback and attentional focus: Enhancing the learning of sport skills through external-focus feedback. *Journal of Motor Behavior, 34,* 171-182.

Wulf, G., & McNevin, N.H. (2003). Simply distracting learners is not enough: More evidence for the learning benefits of an external focus of attention. *European Journal of Sport Science, 3*(5): 1-13.

Wulf, G., McNevin, N.H., Fuchs, T., Ritter, F., & Toole, T. (2000). Attentional focus in complex motor skill learning. *Research Quarterly for Exercise and Sport, 71,* 229-239.

Wulf, G., McNevin, N.H., & Shea, C.H. (2001). The automaticity of complex motor skill learning as a function of attentional focus. *Quarterly Journal of Experimental Psychology, 54A,* 1143-1154.

Wulf, G., Mercer, J., McNevin, N.H., & Guadagnoli, M.A. (2004). Reciprocal influences of attentional focus on postural and supra-postural task performance. *Journal of Motor Behavior, 36,* 189-199.

Wulf, G., & Schmidt, R.A. (1989). The learning of generalized motor programs: Reducing the relative frequency of knowledge of results enhances memory. *Journal of Experimental Psychology: Learning, Memory, and Cognition, 15,* 748-757.

Wulf, G., Schmidt, R.A., & Deubel, H. (1993). Reduced feedback frequency enhances generalized motor program learning but not parameterization learning. *Journal of Experimental Psychology: Learning, Memory, and Cognition, 19,* 1134-1150.

Wulf, G., & Shea, C.H. (2002). Principles derived from the study of simple motor skills do not generalize to complex skill learning. *Psychonomic Bulletin and Review, 9,* 185-211.

Wulf, G., & Shea, C.H. (2004). Understanding the role of augmented feedback: The good, the bad, and the ugly. In A.M. Williams & N.J. Hodges (Eds.), *Skill acquisition in sport: Research, theory and practice* (pp. 121-144). London: Routledge.

Wulf, G., Shea, C.H., & Park, J.H. (2001). Attention in motor learning: Preferences for and advantages of an external focus. *Research Quarterly for Exercise and Sport, 72,* 335-344.

Wulf, G., Töllner, T., & Shea, C.H. (in press). Attentional focus effects as a function of task complexity. *Research Quarterly for Exercise and Sport.*

Wulf, G., Wächter, S., & Wortmann, S. (2003). Attentional focus in motor skill learning: Do females benefit from an external focus? *Women in Sport and Physical Activity Journal, 12,* 37-52.

Wulf, G., & Weigelt, C. (1997). Instructions about physical principles in learning a complex motor skill: To tell or not to tell. . . . *Research Quarterly for Exercise and Sport, 68,* 362-367.

Wulf, G., Weigelt, M., Poulter, D.R., & McNevin, N.H. (2003). Attentional focus on supra-postural tasks affects balance learning. *Quarterly Journal of Experimental Psychology, 56,* 1191-1211.

Wulf, G., Zachry, T., Granados, C., & Dufek, J.S. (2007). Increases in jump-and-reach height through an external focus of attention. *Journal of Sports Science & Coaching, 2,* 275-284.

Yoder, R.M., Nelson, D.L., & Smith, D.A. (1989). Added purpose versus rote exercise in female nursing home residents. *American Journal of Occupational Therapy, 43,* 581-586.

Zachry, T. (2005). Effects of attentional focus on kinematics and muscle activation patterns as a function of expertise. Master's thesis, University of Nevada, Las Vegas.

Zachry, T., Wulf, G., & Mercer, J. (2005). Increases in jump-and-reach height through an external focus of attention. Manuscript submitted for publication.

Zachry, T., Wulf, G., & Mercer, J. , & Bezodis, N. (2005). Increased movement accuracy and reduced EMG activity as the result of adopting an external focus of attention. *Brain Research Bulletin, 67,* 304-309.

INDEX

Note: The italicized *f* and *t* following page numbers refer to figures and tables, respectively.

ABOUT THE AUTHOR

Gabriele Wulf, PhD, is a professor in the department of kinesiology at the University of Nevada at Las Vegas. Dr. Wulf has more than 100 publications in motor learning and control and 35 publications related to attentional focus and motor skills. She initiated the line of research described in this book—external versus internal focus of attention—in the mid-1990s. She has been a section editor for *Research Quarterly for Exercise and Sport* and *Women in Sport and Physical Activity Journal* and has been an editorial board member for *Journal of Motor Behavior, Human Movement Science,* and *International Journal of Fitness,* as well as an international advisory board Member for *Physiotherapy.* She also served as secretary and treasurer from 2002 to 2004 for the North American Society for the Psychology of Sport and Physical Activity.

In her leisure time, Dr. Wulf enjoys working out, skiing, windsurfing, scuba diving, and riding her motorcycle.